Male Survivors

12-Step Recovery Program For
Survivors of Childhood Sexual Abuse

———◆———

With Exercises for Personal Growth

Timothy L. Sanders, MS

 The Crossing Press, Freedom, CA 95019

A Note:

Some of the sections within this book contain material which may be upsetting to adult survivors of childhood abuse.

Some of the names within this text have been changed to ensure anonymity.

The term "Higher Power" will be used in a generic sense for "God" whenever possible. While an individual's understanding of a Higher Power is valid in either feminine, masculine or non-gender forms, the masculine form will be used in this text for the sake of consistency.

Library of Congress Cataloging-on-House Publication Data

Sanders, Timothy L.
    Male Survivors: 12-Step Recovery Program for Survivors of
    Childhood Sexual Abuse / Timothy L. Sanders.
                    p. cm.
    Includes bibliographical references.
    ISBN 0-89594-486-3(cloth) — ISBN 0-89594-485-5(pbk.)
    1. Adult child sexual abuse victims—Rehabilitation—United States.
    2. Twelve-step programs—United States. 3. Boys—United States—
    Abuse of—Psychological aspects. 4. Men—United States—
    Psychology. I. Title.
HQ72.U53S26 1991   91-25384
362.7'6--dc20   CIP

For Kati, my wife who walks beside me, for helping me say "Yes" to the lessons taught by Love, Courage, and Joy.
For Bill and Edith, my parents who believe my story, for helping me say "Yes" to the lessons taught by Faith and Trust.
For the Monks at the Abbey of Gethsemani, my Brothers who offer me Sanctuary, for helping me say "Yes" to the lessons taught by Solitude and Silence.

ACKNOWLEDGMENTS

To Kati Bowen for being so many things to me: wife, partner, confidant, assistant editor, financial consultant, critic, and most precious of all, my best friend. I will always be grateful to you for being there when I have been scattered, confused, worried, anxious, and just plain lost.

Words can never convey the heartfelt gratitude I feel towards all monks at The Abbey of Gethsemani for their prayerful intercessions and compassionate support. I would like to offer a special prayer of thanks for both Father Damian and Brother Luke. Your openhanded welcome has always been warm, the rooms quiet, and the food superb. I am deeply grateful to Brother Patrick Hart for reviewing the embryonic beginnings of this book and helping me to find my voice as a writer. To Brother Anthony Distefano for all the many references, wise encouragement, clear guidance, and our morning meditations together.

To my parents, who not only support me in my Recovery, but who also have had the great courage to walk this path with me. The good gifts you have given have been given to many more than you can ever know.

Thanks to Jerry Johnson, executive director at the Marshall-Jackson Mental Health Center, for graciously allowing me the time off to finish this book. Thanks as well to the secretarial staff who juggled my ever-changing schedule and helped me to keep up with the paperwork: Carolyn Cobb, Cathy Davis, Lori Gray, Norma Helms, Tammy Ivy, and Joyce Jenkins. To my colleagues Dr. Mary Traynor, Leo Pelzel, Jane Waites, and Maura Carter for picking up the slack while I was at home writing. A very special thanks to my friend and former supervisor, Bob Broadfoot, for your unwavering support throughout the past years. You always made the impossible just a little bit easier.

To my former therapist Betty Giardini for being there for me when the memories first returned and later Frank Preston for encouraging me to challenge the shame.

To Father John Groff for your gentle wisdom. To Bill Aycock for rescuing me when the hard disc on the computer crashed! To Clere Englebert of Opening Books for helping me to find a publisher as well as tracking down all the many book orders. To Marie Garrett at the Scottsboro Public Library for keeping up with those strange and peculiar titles coming in on inter-library loan.

Special thanks to Sally Cleveland who taught me to write, Bill Shafer who taught me to trust, and Ray Helms who taught me to feel. To Gini Stone of Hospice of Northeast Alabama who taught me how to do a good job of grieving, and healing. To Carolyn Sneed of NAMI (The National Alliance for the

Mentally Ill) who supported me so many years ago as I took those first tentative steps towards dealing with my past. Likewise, thanks to all the members of the NAMI Sibling and Adult Children Network for enabling me to follow my own path.

I would like to offer a special thanks to Mike Lew for taking the time out of an incredibly busy schedule one weekend to encourage me when I began this book, offering to give me an earful about the 7th Step, answering my phone calls, and having the courage to write *Victims No Longer*. To Hank Estrada, executive director of PLEA (Prevention, Leadership, Education, Assistance) for the correspondence, newsletters, suggested reading lists, and making my own Recovery easier by simply being there.

To all my many friends who have always given more than you will ever know. Sometimes it has taken me years to recognize the gifts which were given so freely. As I think of you all, there is one lesson which keeps coming back: love in this universe is never, ever, wasted. Thanks for the love.

Finally, and by no means the least, thanks to John Gill, Mindy Storch, and the staff at The Crossing Press for your infinite patience and steady guidance as I have struggled with this text. I will always be grateful to you for your willingness to take a risk on the subject which many others were unable to face.

Contents

Preface	The Problem	1
Introduction	The Need for the 12 Steps	3
Chapter 1	The 12 Steps Outlined	7
Chapter 2	The 12 Step Recovery Team and the Goals of Recovery	9
Chapter 3	The Recovery Journal	16
Chapter 4	The 12 Steps Expanded	21
	Step 1 — Acknowledgment	22
	Step 2 — Belief	36
	Prayers for Recovery	45
	Step 3 — Awareness	48
	Step 4 — Self-Examination	81
	Step 5 — Admission	93
	Step 6 — Healing	99
	Step 7 — Forgiveness	126
	Step 8 — Specifying Offences	139
	Step 9 — Making Amends	150
	Step 10 — Daily Growth	161
	Step 11 — Seeking Serenity, Courage, and Wisdom	168
	Step 12 — New Life	174
Epilogue	Life After the 12 Steps	181
Notes		183
Support Groups		185
Suggested Readings		186

---◆---

The Problem

We are scared.
We have difficulties with drugs and alcohol.
We often panic for no reason.
We have trouble with our careers and in our jobs.
We withdraw from intimate relationships, others, the world, and reality.
We deceive ourselves, and then others, about our anxieties and problems.

Our sleep is disturbed, or haunted by nightmares.
Our sexuality causes us confusion and pain,
rather than security and pleasure.
Our lives are out of control, and headed into oblivion.

Stability, calmness, and serenity are foreign realities to us.
Emotional, physical, spiritual, and social pain are daily experiences, and
we do not know why. At times we do not even know we are hurting.

Something always seems to be wrong with us—it is.
Somewhere in the past something happened to us as children
which should not have happened.
Somewhere in the past someone did something to us
he or she should not have done and he/she hurt us.
Someone sexually abused us when we were children.

Our problem is we are adult male survivors of childhood sexual abuse.
Our problem is that we are Men of the Wounded Child.

Introduction

◆

The Need for the 12 Steps
of Recovery

**Life does not count by years. Some suffer
a lifetime in a day, and so grow old
between the rising and the setting of the sun.**
— Augusta Evans

When I look at myself in the mirror I quite naturally see my own reflection. If I look beyond the apparent image, another face comes into focus, an image from the past. I begin to see in the silvered glass the child I once was, the child who still lives within.[1] For some men, the image of their inner child brings forth feelings of secure warmth and delicious joy. For others, like myself, emotions from the past are more haunted, dark and disturbing. For us, these other men, our child knows the realities of intense pain, overwhelming fear, paralyzing rage, and sickening shame. For us the image in the mirror is that of a young boy wounded by the trauma of childhood sexual abuse. We are the men of the wounded child.

For ten years I was sexually abused by my older, adopted brother.

I never knew when my bedroom door would silently open and he would find me, no matter how well I hid myself under the bed or in the closet. He became decidedly sadistic. He tortured me. He brought his friends to use me. I was never safe from him until his escalating violence became intolerable and my parents demanded he leave our home.

Writing or talking about my being sexually abused is still acutely difficult and painful. I still have an overwhelming fear of knives and I still freeze when I hear what I can only describe as "that crazy insane laugh." I am just now beginning to regain the voice I lost through so many years of being completely mute about the abuse.[2]

This book is both a guide for Recovery and a tangible memorial to those of us who did not make the journey from victim to survivor in this life. Through the help of my Higher Power, I have been given the 12 Steps as a pathway for learning to live beyond the traumas of the past: a methodology to rediscover my true and whole self, and the means to begin healing the wounded child within.

Working through the chaos caused by childhood sexual abuse is not easy; it is damn hard work. Facing the past is frightening. With the help of our Higher Power, the miracle of healing can and does happen.

In healing we need some way of communicating and in this fashion, the 12 Steps are especially helpful. Family or friends want to be of assistance; however, they may also be confused by our actions, or even threatened by the changes. Through the 12 Steps you can explain to them where you are in your own Recovery and make it easier to tell them your thoughts and feelings. If these people understand the situation they will be less frightened and defensive. As you become aware of those things you can do to heal your inner child, you can more effectively ask for help. Answers to the long-mysterious questions of "Why...?" will be easier to find.

Like the goal of a good doctor, the goal of the 12 Step Recovery Program is to "put itself out of business." Ultimately, living fully is not something you work at but rather just something you do.

Before continuing any further, we need a working definition of sexual abuse, which is not an easy task. At times there is no question at all as to what constitutes sexual abuse. In other circumstances, it is not so easy to recognize the boundaries between verbal, physical, emotional, sexual and spiritual abuse. If you suspect you were abused as a child, then in all probability you were. In the context of this book a sexually abusive act will be defined as: 1) any sexual act which is not age appropriate for that specific individual to experience or to perform, and 2) any sexual act involving any form of manipulation, coercion, or deliberate force.

It is very easy to deny the daily reality of abusive events in our world and in our own homes. It is the collective social denial which has permitted abuse to happen and to continue.[3] It is denial of these realities on the personal level which blocks true healing. If you are a survivor of sexual abuse your adult denial is rooted in childhood. Not only is this denial a part of the overall abuse syndrome, but it was the key to survival. When you were abused there was no safe way of letting the truth be known. The abuser may have made threats of reprisal, and telling the truth would have placed you and others in real danger. Instinctively you knew these threats to be real. Realize how much courage, faith, creativity, strength, power, genius, and pure guts it took for the little boy on the inside of you simply to hold on from day to day.

Your past feelings of hopelessness are also based on a broader reality.

Years ago there were few resources available for healing. If you had told someone, he or she might not have believed you, or blamed you for "allowing" the abuse. If someone had believed you, what could he or she have done? In the Recovery Process, timing is just as important as technique. The worlds of psychology and social work have undergone profound and sweeping changes within the last decades. We now acknowledge the reality of childhood sexual abuse and affirm the innocence of the victims.[4]

In my own case, I experienced the shame of being sexually abused and the shame of having a mentally ill family member. Samuel, my adopted brother, was eventually diagnosed as suffering a serious psychiatric disorder, further complicated by extensive brain damage from a senseless accident. He is a resident in a state facility for the mentally disabled, where he most likely will remain the rest of his life.

I do not assert that all emotionally disturbed individuals are automatically sexual offenders. In reality they are much more likely to become victims because of their psychiatric problems and poor judgment. Nor are all abusers mentally ill. Frequently the abuser is undeniably rational and responsible for his or her actions. With roots in the modern women's movement, serious study of sexual abuse in childhood and the effects upon adult female survivors has only begun in the past few years.[5] The issue of adult male survivors has remained almost entirely untouched within psychological literature. Hopefully, this book will help eliminate this grievous omission. There is so much we simply do not know. There is so much we have yet to learn. These pages contain points for consideration and further investigation.

This work is based primarily upon my own experiences in Recovery as an adult survivor and those insights provided by my training in counseling and by members of my Recovery Team. The answer to the question, "Does it work?", is the acid test for any tool. I hope and pray that reading these pages proves as powerful a tool for healing for you as writing them has been, and continues to be, for me.

Chapter One

◆

The 12 Steps of Recovery Outlined

Step 1 - Acknowledgment. We acknowledge as children we were powerless over the reality of our being sexually abused. We acknowledge as a result of this past abuse our adult lives have become unmanageable.

Step 2 - Belief. We come to believe a power greater than ourselves can heal our inner, wounded child. We come to believe this Higher Power (as we understand Him) can heal us from the effects childhood sexual abuse has had upon our adult lives.

Step 3 - Awareness. We become aware of how this abuse has had a powerful influence upon our lives and how it has controlled us.

Step 4 - Self-Examination. We make a searching and courageous inventory of how sexual abuse has influenced our life and relationships, both now and in the past.

Step 5 - Admission. We admit to our Higher Power, to ourselves, and to another person the exact nature of how sexual abuse has influenced our life and relationships both now and in the past.

Step 6 - Healing. We willingly ask our Higher Power to heal our pains due to abuse and to free us from the effects these pains continue to have upon our adult lives.

Step 7 - Forgiveness. We humbly ask our Higher Power to forgive us of our shortcomings with ourselves and others caused by childhood abuse and adult patterns of denial.

Step 8 - Specifying Amends. We make a list of all persons we may have harmed as a result of our having been abused. We become willing to make amends to them all.

Step 9 - Making Amends. We make amends to those persons we have harmed or victimized, except when to do so would injure them, others, or ourselves. We also make amends to ourselves.

Step 10 - Daily Growth. We continue to take a daily personal inventory, and when we have been in error we promptly admit it.

Step 11 - Seeking Serenity, Courage and Wisdom. We seek through prayer and meditation to improve conscious contact with our Higher Power, asking only for knowledge of His will for us in our adult lives.

Step 12 - New Life. Having had an adult spiritual awakening as a result of these Steps we try to carry to others our message of New Life through Healing. As a result of this awakening we try to practice the principals of strength, power, gentleness, and forgiveness with others in all our affairs.

Chapter Two

◆

The 12 Step Recovery Team and The Goals of Recovery

The seasons have changed
And the light
And the weather
And the hour.
But it is the same land.
And I begin to know the map
And to get my bearings.
—*Dag Hammarskjöld*

In many untold ways, childhood sexual abuse has influenced all aspects of our adult lives. In order to appreciate what it is like to be inside the mind and soul of an adult male survivor, allow yourself to enter the following drama.

As you awaken each dawn from a fitful night's sleep you find the world much as it was when you went to bed. At least the nightmare you had was only a dream; that is, if you have slept at all. You desperately want your life to be going forward, getting better. Others seem to enjoy life and living. The ordinary things they do look so effortless. Yet, decisions confuse you. Relationships are often complicated and uncomfortable. Depression haunts you. Imagining the future seems so pointless. You sometimes wonder where you are headed. No one knows how much effort it takes just to keep moving and in control. All the while, though, you smile, never letting on to anyone your inner suspicion that something, somewhere, is wrong with you.

One day, however, you gradually begin to realize your life is not running along the straight line you had always thought it was. Reality now seems to be fraying at the edges. Life is beginning to spiral downward uncontrollably in ever-shrinking circles. No matter how hard you struggle to push away your problems with school, work, finances, sexuality, others, and God, they just keep coming back. Not only are the same pains and difficulties recurring more often, but these troubles are also becoming more intense. Your days become heavier and thicker; your thoughts muddier and more unsettling.

You look to friends to help drive away the loneliness, but the part of you which always feels in exile later returns. Lovers supply comfort and sexual release, but this, too, is only a temporary solace. The words of teachers feed the mind, but not your soul. Pastors give what they can, but even their best sage advice never quite fills the empty inner void. You turn to therapists and a host of others for help with your problems, but, one by one, each of these outward saviors fails to grant the solution which will finally end the gnawing inward aches. Drugs and alcohol numb the mind and kill the pain, at least for a while. However, there still is the next day, the next week, the next year to be faced, and endured. Despite all your efforts at eliminating the growing insanity, life continues to become more complicated, and you do not know why. Finally, you awaken to the uneasy truth you are stuck in an emotional wasteland. The idea of suicide takes on an alluring appeal. You do not want to even think about being lost in this place, this middle of nowhere. Yet, awareness rises to the surface of your conscious mind from the depths of your being like quiet whispers which will not go away.

"What you remember as your past is not your past . . ."
"What you thought were your problems is not your real problem . . ."
"Where you believed you have been is not where you have been at all . . ."
"Who you thought you were is not who you truly are . . ."
"The land you are living in is an illusion . . ."
"You are lost, and you have been lost for years . . ."

Deep in your bones there is a horrible truth you have been carrying around within yourself. Denial will no longer stifle memories of things seen, heard, smelled and felt. Finally, you cry out from the very depths of your being the words you can no longer repress:

"HE RAPED ME!"
"SHE MOLESTED ME!"
"THEY MADE ME DO THINGS!"
"I WAS SEXUALLY ABUSED!!"

After this wrenching awareness, what next? If there is no clear means of healing your inner wounded child, no clear path home toward wholeness, it would be very seductive to go back to living in that nowhere land of denial and self-deception. If you have no map, no compass, no road, no guide, and find no sanctuary, why even begin? If you do not know your destination, why should you go on living? You need a map! You need a reason to live! The 12 Steps can be that map and that reason!

For a number of years it has been recognized in cases of childhood sexual abuse that no one person or single method of treatment could realistically be expected to be the single resource necessary for healing and recovery. The issues are too complicated. The effects too diverse. It was out of this recognition the use of "The Team Approach" developed. Now it is common for a team of specialists from a number of different disciplines such as psychology, social work, education, medicine, and physical therapy to be brought together to help heal the child and the family. Together they address the causes, effects and prevention of sexual abuse on a case-by-case basis. In many places, it is considered poor practice, or even unethical, not to use the team approach. For adult male survivors who will be using the 12 Steps, I also strongly recommend the use of the Recovery Team. In fact, I will go so far as to say it both dangerous and unwise not to assemble such a group of people around you as you begin the Recovery Process.

Within the context of this book, in addition to the 12 Step Recovery Process, we will use six broad headings or Life Areas to organize and direct our Recovery. These six Life Areas are: Psychological, Spiritual, Sexual, Physical, Social, and Economic. To form your Recovery Team you might choose some-one for each Life Area. These various parts of our lives are not separate and distinct, but intimately connected. Whether we realize it or not, what happens in one portion of our lives ultimately influences all the other parts of our being. Because of the overlap of the six Life Areas, it is possible for one team member to help with several different aspects of living. However, it is impossible for any one person to help you effectively deal with them all. If you expect any one team member to be all things to you at all times, you are setting yourself up for more disappointment and hurt. Therefore, be kind to your inner self and treat this part of you with sanity and love. Give to your wounded inner child only the best resources you can find by putting together a good Recovery Team.

Books and various writers can also be used as members of your Recovery Team. Through the gifts of technology, it is now possible for us at the cost of less than a meal and a glass of wine to tap into the hearts and minds of some of the greatest healers, spiritual guides and teachers both from the past, and of the present. Their wisdom is truly at our fingertips. We only have to be willing to seek out their written words in order to discover what they have to say to us. A listing of recommended readings for each Life Area can be found at the end of this book.

To begin developing your 12 Step Recovery Team, keep in mind the six broad aspects of your life which have been affected by sexual abuse. In the following section under each Life Area, suggestions are provided for the types of individuals who may be able to help. As you examine these suggestions, begin to think about those individuals who may be already available to you. When specific people, groups, or books come to mind start to list them on the page provided at the end of this chapter.

Psychological: Psychiatrist, psychologist, professional counselor, or licensed social worker.

The goal of Recovery in this Life Area is to reclaim the full use of your mind and your feelings, and to integrate the fragmented components of your personality. Emotional healing helps you to break free from self-destructive patterns of re-victimization. The task of working through the layers of denial, confusion, conflict, anger, rage, and pain is often difficult and frightening.

Many times feelings of hopelessness and despair will creep in only to freeze your Recovery in mid-stride. Recognize this as another effect of the abuse. Do not stop your efforts, because the result of cleansing the mind of these infected wounds is the liberation of your inner child. You would not expect a child to be free from the effects of such a trauma overnight or even within a matter of weeks or months. Therefore, do not expect your own Recovery to happen immediately. Through this work, you will discover the forgotten joys of creative thinking, unfettered play, and childlike wonderment. You will begin to trust your own intuitions, and you will develop self-appreciation. In selecting someone to help you in this area, there is one simple rule: find someone you know you can trust, and with whom you feel safe.

Spiritual: Pastor, rabbi, priest, retreat director, or meditation instructor.

The recovery goal here is to re-awaken the spiritual relationship you had with your Higher Power which seemed to disappear the moment you were sexually abused. For many years, you may have believed in your heart the Lie that your Higher Power abandoned you; He allowed this to happen; or He did this to you Himself. The Truth is this spiritual relationship was never totally severed, though, at times, it may have felt that way.

Joining a religious organization or latching onto a spiritual guru does not automatically make you a spiritual pilgrim. Examine your own religious tradition; you might want to begin your journey there. Be open to what fellow travelers from other traditions have to say to you on your path. It does not matter from where you begin your pilgrimage. What matters is that you get started.

Sexual: Sex therapist, partner, lover, or spouse.

The recovery goal here is to allow you to celebrate the entire range of sensual, erotic, and orgasmic experiences. As a whole man, you can free yourself from the negative associations sexuality has had for you in the past. As an adult, you can reclaim your right to experience your sexual self. Through Recovery, you are given permission to empower the part of you which can experience sexuality as a joyous gift full of tenderness, strength, gentleness, passion, security, and pleasure. You no longer need associate sexual activity with brutality, confusion, powerlessness, cruelty, fear, and pain. As you integrate your mind, body, and soul, the Recovery Process will allow you to discover entirely new levels of intimacy and sharing.

Physical: Licensed body or massage therapist, martial arts teacher, physical therapist, athletic consultant, yoga instructor, dietitian, or certified chemical dependency treatment counselor.

Here the goal is to release those past pains which have been buried in the muscles and fibers of your body. In doing so, you will begin to listen to the messages your body now sends. You will also start to claim the wellness necessary to enjoy, thrive and participate in life. In the past, the denial of your physical pains enabled you to survive, but this denial is now blocking your capacity to experience the pleasures of living.

Just as pushing one domino causes other dominoes to fall, childhood denial causes other forms of denial in adulthood. Current means of maintaining denial may include drugs, alcohol, or sexual escapism. Such coping strategies may have been quite successful in temporarily killing the pain; however, these negative coping patterns can eventually become problems or addictions themselves. Obesity, bulimia, or malnutrition may be the result of a distorted body image. Because of the hopelessness abuse victims commonly feel, you may see no need to prepare yourself for a long life. Self-fulfilling prophecies can be very powerful, even deadly! Healing feeds into more healing. Establishing and strengthening the mind/body connection gives you the power and energy to do the work of Recovery in other Life Areas.

Social: Warm, non-judgmental friends, secure social situations, Recovery support groups, safe environments, and decent housing.

In this aspect of our lives, the Recovery goal is to free ourselves from current fears stemming from the environment in which we were abused. We can give to our inner child loving relationships within a secure environment. We no longer have to run in order to be safe. In the Recovery process, we will be free to come and go as we please with a sense of security. We will no longer be bound by childhood fears.

Through the effects of denial, we continually find ourselves experiencing painful relationships. This is because of our blind pattern of looking for others to heal our inner wounds. When these people failed to end our pains, we became angry at them and, eventually, at ourselves. We thought we were going forward, but, in reality, we were just going around in circles. As we go within to heal ourselves, we will no longer hold such unrealistic expectations of others. Because of our willingness to give good things to our inner child, we will begin to find we deserve loving, kind, warm, and supportive relationships. Our Recovery will also show us we deserve a decent, secure place to live.

Economic: Career consultant, vocational rehabilitation counselor, academic advisor, accountant, financial advisor, or estate planner.

The goal in this Life Area is to help you see that you truly do deserve financial security. You actually do have the power to make wise adult financial decisions. However, Recovery is not cheap. You may need some assistance here to ensure that the cost of your Recovery does not make your life more complicated. How much money can you realistically afford to dedicate to your Recovery on a weekly, monthly, or yearly basis? While your wounded inner child requires healing, he also needs good food to eat, a warm bed in which to sleep, and comfortable clothes to wear. Take care of the basics first, and go from there.

Another aspect of Recovery in this area involves an examination of your source of income. Is your career based upon your true talents and gifts, or is it based upon an overriding need for security? A part of your long-term recovery could involve a job change, a career switch, additional education, or even retraining.

Those healthy, growing people whom you place on your Recovery Team tend to surround themselves with healthy growing friends, associates, and acquaintances. They have had their own struggles to contend with, and they work at finding new solutions to new problems, or even using old solutions in new ways. If you can find even one good person to be on your Recovery Team, then it is probable this person knows of other resources to aid you. Be willing to take advantage of those networks the members of your Recovery Team have established. Some team members may be with you for years, or even for a lifetime; whereas, other members may be active in your Recovery for only a short time, leaving once their job is finished. As you change throughout your Recovery, your needs will also change. The emphasis upon the various Life Areas will, as a matter of course, ebb and flow. Thus, allow your Recovery Team to change. Give yourself permission to evolve.

In reviewing your list of team members, realize in certain circumstances you will need to clearly explain to them you are a recovering adult survivor of childhood sexual abuse, and you are following a 12 Step Recovery Program. You will also need to openly communicate to them how you want them to help you. This is especially true in the Psychological, Sexual, Physical and Spiritual Life Areas. At that point, they can tell you what they can or cannot do to help you. Do not be offended if any one of them refers you on to someone else. Trust their judgment about their own skills. There are no hard and fast rules concerning self-disclosure. If there is doubt on your part concerning this matter, then go gently with yourself.

12 Step Recovery Team Members

Psychological

_____
_____
_____
_____

Spiritual

_____
_____
_____
_____

Sexual

_____
_____
_____
_____

Physical

_____
_____
_____
_____

Social

_____
_____
_____
_____

Economic

_____
_____
_____
_____

Chapter Three

◆

The Recovery Journal

The most difficult thing in life
is to know yourself.
— *Thales*

Anyone who uses the 12 Step Recovery Program should give serious thought to keeping a Recovery Journal. This special journal will help us to focus daily in written form upon our private personal responses to the world as we begin to listen to and to heal our wounded, inner child. In many ways, our Recovery Journal can be seen both as an archaeological record and as a scientific laboratory report. In our Journal, we collect information about our current lives. We then develop ideas about why certain things are or are not working. Finally, we note the results of our experiments in living. In it, we also explore our past as we sift through the layers of our personal history searching for insights about ourselves. Because of childhood sexual abuse, the wholeness we once possessed has become lost and scattered. Our Recovery Journal helps us to find anew those parts of our selves which are missing. It leads us to where we need to go to find them. Once found, these lost pieces can then be re-established in their proper place. The 12 Steps help us to rediscover the completeness of spirit, body and mind which is our birthright.

In my own journey towards healing, I have found the use of a journal to be one of the most powerful tools available for working the 12 Steps. It is also one of the simplest for it is nothing more than a pad of paper, a pen, and a quiet place to write. I began journal writing while in my early twenties as a means of trying to gain some insight into my recurrent fall depressions, as well as my chronic battles with emotional, spiritual, and sexual confusion. Shortly after initiating this journal, I came across the writings of Ira Progoff. In his book, *At*

A Journal Workshop, he offers a carefully developed and powerful method for journal writing.[1]

Because I suffered from sleep disturbances and recurrent nightmares, keeping a Dream Log seemed a logical thing to do to help me develop some sense of what these night terrors meant, if they meant anything at all. I am now convinced these dreams did have something to say and believe they played an important role in leading up to the breakthrough of my recalling the sexual abuse I experienced in childhood. Within the previous decade, I had entered into psychotherapy four times but it was only in the fifth course of counseling that I focused upon the content of these dreams.

Several months after entering therapy, my supervisor gave me a copy of Stephen LeBarge's book, *Lucid Dreaming*.[2] This work is a compilation of clear theories and simple techniques which can be used to allow one to obtain the apparently paradoxical state of being awake, or conscious, while dreaming. Such techniques teach an individual how to directly manipulate the content of their dreams, thereby working through those unconscious fears and conflicts which cause these troubling dreams in the first place.

After I began to recall my childhood abuse, I reviewed the journal writings I had kept over the previous ten years. In doing so, I was shocked to find among those thousands of entries I had mentioned my adopted brother Samuel only three times. I pulled out what I thought might be helpful to me in the future, and burned the rest. The night I ritually set fire to those discarded entries and the four large boxes they filled, I vowed to myself, no matter what the cost, I would not spend the remaining years of my life being as blind, and as lost, as I had been in the past.

In organizing your Recovery Journal, I would suggest you include at least two specific sections. The first of these is that portion committed to the Daily Journal. The second section is dedicated to each of the 12 Steps, or a 12 Step Recovery Journal. The particulars of the 12 Steps are explored in greater detail later in this work. Beyond these two basic and necessary divisions, you may consider the option of employing a Dream Log. The following comments about keeping both a Daily and a 12 Step Recovery Journal are a distillation of those techniques which I have found to be most useful.

There is only one certain rule for keeping a Recovery Journal: use what works for you. We often panic when faced with a blank sheet of paper in front of us for the first time as we begin our writing. We feel we have nothing to say. We have no answers for we do not even know the questions. One means of avoiding this initial sense of frustration and anxiety is to place a copy of the 12 Steps at the very front of your Journal. You can then easily use the Steps as a starting point at any time to help you organize your thoughts.

Whether you select loose-leaf, bound, lined, colored, or plain paper, make sure it is pleasing to your eye. Find a pen or pencil that feels good in your hand. Give yourself a fine leather notebook or ledger pad. Spend a little extra money on these things. You are making an investment in yourself of both time and effort, so give your inner child the best materials you can. Once you have gathered your tools of paper and pen together you need to find a quiet time and place to actually do your journal work. Think about when you are able to find silence and solitude during your day. Some individuals learn morning is best for them while others discover their best writing time is late at night. Regardless of the specific time of day you choose, make certain this time is yours and only yours. Leave the television off, and keep the radio hushed. You might want to unplug the phone. If someone knocks on the door, tell them you are busy now, and you will get back with them later.

The place where you write is important as well. Again, experiment with several different places until you find the one place where your inner child feels most comfortable. Sit down in several different locations throughout the house until you find a spot which feels right. Re-arrange the furniture if you need to or keep the doors locked. Some folks will find a kitchen table with a hot cup of coffee helps them to collect and focus upon their thoughts. Others will use a desk in their study, or maybe a chair in front of a window with a quiet view. When the weather is temperate try the patio, porch, city park, or empty woods. Sometimes to find a safe place you may need to leave the house altogether and go elsewhere such as the library, a quiet coffee shop, a hotel room, a friend's house, or even a retreat facility.

Having found your time and place to write, make it a habit of going there regularly. Not all habits are bad! You will find as you return to your special place that it will become easier and more natural for you to do your journal writing, and listen to the child within.

While there is no absolutely right way of keeping either your Daily or your 12 Step Recovery Journal, there are four specific attitudes you will find helpful. The first pair of these attitudes is Patience and Commitment. Be patient if no miracles happen within the first week or two. It took more than a couple of days for you to get to where you are now. In fact, it took your entire lifetime to reach this point! Realize it will take some time, but not forever, for you to move out from your present conflicts, confusion and turmoil into a healthier, safer and more comfortable place. In those times when you find yourself with nothing to say, remain committed to the 12 Steps and your Recovery Journal. A good suggestion for those days when you are short of words is to go to the next blank page and write down the date followed by, "I have nothing to say today . . ." You may even have days or weeks during which the words simply will not come. Remember these fallow times almost always precede periods of growth and insight for Recovery follows a path marked by empty plateaus and healing inclines.

The second set of helpful attitudes is Honesty and Courage. When you say, "Well, I should not feel this or that," or "I must not think those kind of thoughts," and then do not go ahead and write them down, no matter what they are, you are only being dishonest with yourself. Sometimes it takes courage to write out on paper what is happening up in your head, down in your heart, and deep in your guts. If you are afraid someone will somehow read that which you are ashamed or afraid to write, go ahead and write it down anyway. When you are through, you can always pull this page from your journal and burn it. The important thing to remember is that you got it out of your system.

After you actively begin your Recovery there are three things you can expect to have happen. The first of these is an increased awareness of your own thoughts and feelings. These inner reactions to outer circumstances and events will be from both the past and present. Now that you have taken the time to listen to your inner child, you will find he really does have something to say.

Secondly, you will begin to perceive the daily, weekly, monthly, and yearly patterns present in your life. More often than not, the difficulties people experience are circular in nature. This is especially true if those major, core issues were not successfully resolved at an earlier time. Symptoms of chronic sexual confusion, depression, panic, anger, relationship problems, nightmares, financial difficulties, or drug or alcohol addiction may be due to the effects of childhood abuse.

It is only when the person with these symptoms begins to actively explore and to consciously note the broader parts of his life from the past, and in the present, that these symptoms then fall into their proper place. This person's real problem may be that he is not giving himself time to be alone with his wounded, inner child. Maybe he is trying to kill off his child's pain rather than listen to it. Maybe he is trying to solve everyone else's problems in a vain hope of solving his own. Maybe he has not yet learned to let go.

However, there is a positive side to recurrent life patterns. If our lives begin to go in the directions we wish them to be headed, there are reasons for this, and it is not due to magic or accident. Through the 12 Steps we can more easily recognize specific actions and uncover particular techniques which work for us in our own healing. With this information we can follow the same or similar successful strategies again. Our feelings, both pleasant and unpleasant, do not float in from nowhere.

The final thing you can expect to have happen from your following the Recovery Process is that your vision of the future will begin to change. Through exploring your past and by becoming more aware of your present, the future need no longer be a fearful, unforeseeable road. Apathy will be replaced by hope, and powerlessness will be transfigured into inner strength. You will also discover you have started to find the Serenity to accept the things of the past you cannot change, the Courage to change the things in the present and future you can change, and the Inner Wisdom to know the difference between the two.

Chapter Four

◆

The 12 Steps Expanded

Step 1: Acknowledgment

Step 2: Belief

Step3: Awareness

Step4: Self-examination

Step5: Admission

Step 6: Healing

Step 7: Forgiveness

Step 8: Specifying Amends

Step 9: Making Amends

Step 10: Daily Growth

Step 11: Seeking Serenity,

   Courage and Wisdom

Step 12: New Life

Chapter Four

The 12 Steps Expanded

Step 1

◆

Acknowledgment

We acknowledge as children we were powerless over the reality of our being sexually abused. We acknowledge as a result of this past abuse our adult lives have become unmanageable.

I would strongly suggest you read this chapter through at least once before attempting any of the suggested Step 1 exercises. It is very easy to become lost unless you clearly know where you are headed. Also, make sure you keep handy a list of your Recovery Team members along with their phone numbers. Having them "on stand-by" may prove to be helpful if you start to run into trouble. **However, if at any time you feel that any of this material is becoming too intense for you, please stop! Remember you have the right to stop doing something which either is not good for you, or you do not want to do. If you should suddenly feel depressed, or suicidal, put down the book and call one of your Recovery Team members immediately!**

While acknowledgment may be the first step in Recovery, it is not the beginning. As far as my own story is concerned, I followed many blind alleys until I reached the inescapable truth about my own past.

The exact place and time I first recalled being sexually abused was one week before Christmas after a difficult session with my therapist. During the nights before our session, I had experienced two peculiar and vivid dreams, and we had explored their possible meanings. The first dream involved my successful struggle to stop Samuel from attacking me, and the second pertained to the strangely reassuring image of myself as a Buddhist monk. After I had left my therapist's office, I tried not to think about our session; rather, I attempted to allow the various thoughts, associations, images, and jumbled emotions to settle down and sort themselves out.

Miles outside the city, as I began to climb a steep stretch of road, something down in my guts suddenly "clicked." Everything was now moving in slow motion. I reached down, turned off the radio, lifted my foot off the accelerator, and let the car coast. Before my eyes, just beyond the edge of the windshield, I began to see long-forgotten images from my buried past. What I saw was neither the re-visualization of a dream, nor any hallucination. I had heard of flashbacks before, but now I was having one![1] There before me, in undeniable terms, was the truth that I had been sexually abused.

In looking back at the days, weeks, and months which followed this explosive awareness, I now realize how my reactions paralleled those stages found in any intense grief reaction.[2] Those five stages, modified here for adult survivors, are: Shock-Denial, Rage-Terror, Bargaining, Mourning, and Continued Living. I will be using my own story to illustrate each of these stages.

The Shock-Denial Stage

When I was first sexually assaulted, the boy child I was went into physical, emotional, and psychological shock. For a child's mind to cope with such a trauma was just too much. While the abuse did not kill me, the overload caused a part of my child's psyche to split off and become trapped in denial. With the abuse encapsulated, the remaining portions of my being were able to continue living. Yet, there was left behind an unconscious portion of myself frozen in time, forever re-experiencing the minutes just prior to the actual abuse.[3]

Over the years with each separate instance of forced oral sex or sodomy, an older and slightly different child once again experienced the same pattern of shock, and the same subsequent self-protective denial. As this abuse continued, there developed many buried parts of myself, each trapped in a twisted twilight zone, endlessly re-playing over and over again the separate times leading up to the molestations. However, none of those inner children could ever remember what actually happened next because of the repression. I went into shock.

With those previously separate and lost parts of my being now becoming one, a more integrated self began to remember, and re-live, the past. For years I had been searching for the answers to "Why . . ." Now I had my answer, and I wanted it to be anything other than the one I was given. The old adage of "Be careful what you ask for, you just may get it" took on a macabre tone. All the pieces of the puzzle fit and the truth was undeniable.

The Rage-Terror Stage

Anger does not come close to describing the emotion I felt. I spent hours and days driving in my car with the radio turned up as loud as I could stand it. It did not matter where I was going, all that mattered was that I was moving. Sheer rage was welling up within me and the fear of losing control was paralyzing. December twenty-fifth is Sam's birthday and Christmas was days away. I could not get out of visiting my family, if only for a few hours.

During the previous months, I had made an effort to have almost no contact with my family. I knew if I did not see them over the holidays, they would start asking questions about why I was avoiding them. There was a wiser part of me which knew neither they, nor myself, were ready to deal with the truth. The last thing I needed to do was to unload all of this on everyone in the middle of Christmas dinner. Where were Mom and Dad when I needed them most? Couldn't they tell something was happening to me? They were supposed to protect me, but they did not. What could have been more important than stopping Sam from hurting me? These questions did not come from my adult self, but rather my inner wounded child. Still the rage was there. Also, there was the terror . . .

I never knew when the flashbacks would happen, nor what the nightmares would bring. When either of these occurred, it was as if the abuse were happening all over again with the same original physical responses, along with the same level of emotional intensity. You cannot talk a child out of being angry or scared, and my inner child was filled with rage and terror.

Christmas Eve after attending church services, I headed off to the congregational party at a member's home. While there, I made a serious dent in the fifth of Scotch I brought along. The next morning I had a massive hangover. Somehow I remembered to pack all the gifts. All down the interstate I kept the car at seventy miles an hour, again with the radio tuned into the clearest, and loudest, rock-and-roll station I could find. When I arrived I could tell the family knew something was not right, but no one said anything about it. Early in the afternoon I sensed my defenses were weakening, and I said an abrupt good-bye. Driving home I found myself beating the dashboard as I screamed and cried. The radio will only drown out so much of the noise going on inside your head.

Bargaining

I tried desperately to discount what I had discovered about myself. This bargaining stage led me to question my own sanity. Could I have made this all up? How could I prove what I knew was the truth, since no physical evidence existed? Who will believe me? Why should I even believe myself? However, the inner evidence was still there. The flashbacks during the daytime were too real. The nightmares were no longer symbolic. Even in my sleep I re-lived what had happened so long ago . . .

I see Samuel walking down the hall without any clothes on . . . I am lying on the bed, feeling his weight on top of me . . . He is tickling me and I want him to stop and he does not stop . . . I hear his tongue in my ear as he kisses me . . . I hear Samuel and his friends in the bedroom laughing . . . I hear him call out my name, "Timmy, where are you?" . . . I am hiding under the bed and they find me . . . I am hiding in the closet and they find me . . . I pray to God to make the pain stop . . . I hear him senselessly muttering louder and louder to himself until he reaches orgasm . . . I pray Mom and Dad would come home soon . . . I also remember being horrified at the thought of what might happen if they did come home and find out what was happening . . .and this went on for over ten years . . .

No, the truth was the truth and no amount of bargaining would make it any less so. I tried to find something in the past I could have changed. Desperately, I searched for the one missing piece which would have prevented the sexual assaults. However, I realized one of the most perverse things an adult could ever say is that the abuse is the fault of the victim. If I would not do this to a child, then neither could I do this to myself. I had to face and accept the truth that I was indeed powerless over my having been sexually molested as a child.

Mourning

After the holidays, the grief became intense. All I could do was cry. So many parts of myself had died over the years, and each of these aspects of my life needed to be mourned. Nothing I could do could ever re-write the past. All I had was the future, but there was something about this which bothered me deeply. I began to become aware of the innumerable losses in my life which had accumulated, one upon the other as the years passed. So many of the normal experiences of childhood and adolescence simply never happened and I felt numbed. Those years were now gone forever.

As I continued to become more conscious of the insidious ways early traumas affected my younger years, I also realized how those influences had continued into my adult life. There were the many years of therapy; the phobic responses to enclosed spaces; my compulsive need for control; the driven nature of my spiritual quest; my ever-increasing abuse of alcohol: the list of the effects continued to grow. Finally, I had to acknowledge that my life, at age 30, was out of control. When I was able to admit this to myself, I realized I had finished taking the first step in my own Recovery.

The Continued Living Stage

The final stage in grief work is known as Continued Living. Despite the horrors of the past there is the present, and can be a future. By working the remaining steps of Recovery, the means for this future is found.

> **How can such deep-imprinted images**
> **sleep in us at times, till a word,**
> **a sound, awake them?**
> **— *Lessing***

Exercises for Step One

The following questions are not easy to answer. Some specifically ask for information about where you were abused, how you were abused, and by whom. **If you do choose to answer these questions, answer them only if you are in a safe place and/or surrounded by safe people.** Try to apply yourself to these exercises for no more than half an hour or so. Our attention span typically runs around twenty minutes and beyond that time our ability to concentrate drops off significantly. If you try working longer than this, you will probably not be using your time effectively.

Step One and The Shock-Denial Stage of Recovery

1. How would you rate your present awareness of the facts concerning the abuse?

      Very Aware   Somewhat Aware   Not Aware

How would you rate your current awareness of the emotions you experienced at the time of the abuse?

      Very Aware   Somewhat Aware   Not Aware

2. For adult survivors it is not uncommon for a series of events, or crises, to initiate the breakdown of our denial. If this was your situation, what happened that helped you to begin to move through the denial?

Health problems	_____	Financial problems	_____
Drug or alcohol problems	_____	Legal charges	_____
Birth of child	_____	Child turning a particular age	_____
Psychological problems	_____	Death of friend	_____
Death of family member	_____	Death of the abuser	_____
Getting a new job	_____	Losing an old job	_____
Marriage	_____	Entering a committed relationship	_____
Divorce	_____	End of long-term relationship	_____
Other _____			

3. Often times as adults we will unconsciously do things which help us maintain the denial. This often results in our adult lives' being out of control. Which of the following could be ways that your adult life is now out of control?

work addiction	_____	religious compulsions	_____
drugs or alcohol	_____	sexual acting out	_____
eating disorders	_____	health issues	_____
avoiding relationships	_____	avoiding stability	_____

behavioral addictions (for example: running, exercising, or meditating too much and not being able to stop) _____

Other _____

4. If you can, do you remember where you were sexually abused, or where the abuse happened most often?

house	_____	yard	_____	barn	_____
school	_____	church	_____	car/bus	_____
outdoors	_____	camp	_____	hotel/motel	_____
office	_____	store	_____	library	_____
friend's house	_____	business	_____		

Other _____

5. If you can remember (and it is OK if you do not remember), who sexually abused you as a child? You may check more than one category if you need to do so.

Family member _____   Family friend _____
Church member _____   Neighbor _____
Teacher _____   Stranger _____
Other _____
Do Not Remember _____

6. Was/were the abuser/s: Male _____   Female _____   Both _____

7. Again, if you can remember, at what age or ages were you sexually molested? It is OK if you can only guess at the age. You may check more than one.

Birth to age one _____   Age one to two _____
Age two to four _____   Age four to six _____
Age six to eight _____   Age eight to ten _____
Age ten to twelve _____   Age twelve to fifteen _____
Age fifteen to eighteen _____

8. Do you remember how you were sexually abused?

Yes __ No ___ Maybe ___

If you are willing to name the abuse, which of the following applies to you?

___ You performed oral sex on abuser's genitals.
___ They performed oral sex on your genitals.
___ You performed anal sex with the abuser.
___ They performed anal sex with you.
___ You orally stimulated their anus.
___ They orally stimulated your anus.
___ You stimulated their anus with your hand.
___ They stimulated your anus with their hand.
___ You fondled or masturbated their genitals.
___ They fondled or masturbated your genitals.
___ You fondled their body.
___ They fondled your body.
___ You had sex with other children.
___ You had sex with other adults.
___ Your being in photographs/movies
___ Satanic/Occult rituals
___ Prostitution
___ Sex with animals
Other _____

Step One and The Rage-Terror Stage of Recovery

1. Do you now have, or have you ever had, any of the following?
   ___ Flashbacks (re-experiencing the abuse)
   ___ Intrusive memories (memories that are not sought out)
   ___ Symbolic nightmares of the abuse
   ___ Non-symbolic nightmares of the abuse
   ___ Panic attacks
   ___ Body memories (physically feeling as if the abuse were re-occurring)
   ___ Free-floating fears
   ___ Specific phobic reactions

2. Have you ever suffered from chronic anxiety?
   Yes ___ No ___
If yes, is there a particular time of the year when the anxiety is worse than others?
   Yes ___ No ___ Uncertain ___
If yes, what time of the year is this anxiety worse? You may check more than one if need be.
   Spring ___ Summer ___ Fall ___ Winter ___
Is this the same season, or the season just before or after, when you were sexually abused as a child?
   Yes ___ No ___ No relation ___

3. What do you do when you feel that you are about to lose control of your anger?
   A. _____
   B. _____
Have these behaviors ever caused you any problems or difficulties, or endangered your life or the lives of others?
   Yes ___ No ___ Uncertain ___

4. When you have lost control, what do you do to help you regain your control?
   A. _____
   B. _____
Have these behaviors themselves ever caused you any problems or difficulties or endangered your life?
   Yes ___ No ___ Uncertain ___

5. Have you ever in the past taken your anger out on yourself or others, even if you did not know that you were doing so at the time?

Yes ___ No ___ Uncertain ___

If you have taken out the anger and rage upon yourself or others in the past, how did you do this?

A. _____

B. _____

Step One and The Bargaining Stage of Recovery

1. Have you, or anyone else, ever discounted your memories of the abuse as simply bad dreams, hallucinations, fantasies or lies?

Yes ___ No ___

If you can recall, tell who did this and how your memories were discounted.

A. Who? _____

How? _____

B. Who? _____

How? _____

2. In the past, to what degree did you feel that the abuse was your fault?

All my fault_____Some my fault_____Not my fault at all_____

3. To what degree do you *presently* feel that the abuse was your fault?

All my fault_____Some my fault_____Not my fault at all_____

4. In the past, how much did you feel that you "asked for" the abuse?

I asked for it all _____ I might have asked for some of it _____

I did not ask for any of it _____

5. To what degree do you *presently* feel that you "asked for" the abuse?

I asked for it all _____ I might have asked for some of it _____

I did not ask for any of it _____

6. Were you ever told by the abuser/s not to tell about the abuse?

Yes ___ No ___ Uncertain ___

If yes, what were you told would happen if you did reveal the abuse to anyone?

A. _____

B. _____

7. As a child, what was the worst thing/s that could have happened in your family if the sexual abuse had been revealed? For example: Someone would have been killed.

A. _____

B. _____

8. Did maintaining silence as a child have the positive function of keeping anyone alive, protected or safe from harm?

       Yes ___ No ___ Uncertain ___

If yes, who were these people and how did your silence keep them alive, protected or safe from harm?

      A. Who? _____

           How? _____

      B. Who? _____

           How? _____

Step One and The Mourning Stage of Recovery

1. Have you ever suffered from chronic or recurrent seasonal depression?
Yes ___ No ___
If yes, what is the time of the year when the depression is worse than others?
You may check more than one.
Spring ___ Summer ___ Fall ___ Winter ___
Is this the same season, or the season just before or just after, you were sexually abused as a child?
Yes ___ No ___ Uncertain ___

2. Have you ever suffered from chronic or recurrent depression associated with a particular holiday, celebration, or ongoing family event?
Yes ___ No ___
If yes, what is the holiday, celebration or family event when the depression is worse?
A. _____
B. _____
Is this the same holiday, celebration or family event during which you were sexually abused as a child?
Yes ___ No ___ Uncertain ___

3. Losses include not only those things we once had and no longer possess, but also those things which should have been but never were. Are you now aware of any particular loss which occurred as a result of your childhood sexual abuse? If so, you may find it helpful to write them out below.

Psychological Losses
A. _____
B. _____

Spiritual Losses
A. _____
B. _____

Sexual Losses
A. _____
B. _____

Physical Losses

    A. _____

    B. _____

Social Losses

    A. _____

    B. _____

Economic Losses

    A. _____

    B. _____

4. In reviewing the above list, what losses are you grieving right now? Circle those that are especially difficult for you to cope with.

5. Have you ever talked with anyone about these losses?

    Yes ___ No ___

If no, would you be willing to discuss these losses with a member of your Recovery Team?

    Yes ___ No ___

Step One and The Continued Living
Stage of Recovery

1. As part of your working this Step, you might consider writing within your 12 Step Recovery Journal what helped you recall your childhood sexual abuse. You might consider a title for this entry as "My Story . . ."

2. Also, you might consider writing out within your 12 Step Recovery Journal how you became aware that your adult life was/is out of control. This could be a continuation of the previous entry, this one entitled "My Story Continued . . ."

3. As an alternative to writing out "My Story . . ." or "My Story Continued . . ." you might think about how the Five Stages of Loss listed below apply to you. You might wish to use them as an outline to guide you in writing out this entry in your 12 Step Recovery Journal.
     1. Shock/Denial
     2. Rage/Terror
     3. Bargaining
     4. Mourning
     5. Continued Living

4. What scares you about Continued Living?
    ___ Going crazy
    ___ Confronting my family
    ___ Confronting the abuser
    ___ Telling my friends about the abuse
    ___ Splitting up my family
    ___ Losing my partner or spouse
    ___ Losing my job
    ___ That going through Recovery will kill me
    ___ No one will believe what happened to me
Others fears about Continued Living
    A. _____
    B. _____

Step 2

◆

Belief

**We come to believe a power greater than ourselves can heal
our inner, wounded child. We come to believe this Higher
Power (as we understand Him) can heal us from the effects
childhood sexual abuse has had upon our adult lives.**

For many adult survivors the entire issue of a Higher Power is especially
confusing. This internal conflict often makes taking the 2nd Step very difficult,
if not at times impossible. There are any number of reasons for this dilemma.
The goals of this chapter are to detail the sources of this turmoil in our
relationship to our Higher Power, examine its effects, and then to explore
possible solutions for reestablishing our relationship with Him. I would especially like to credit Father Leonard Loegering for his pioneering contributions
upon how abuse distorts spirituality, especially his "Gut God versus Head God"
conceptualization. Much of this chapter has been inspired by his insights. For
the sake of clarity throughout this section I will be using the term "Church" to
denote any organized spiritual body regardless of religion, denomination,
or sect.

One of the sources of an adult survivor's spiritual confusion is traceable
to the Church's historical failure to confront and address the issue of abuse.
While the Church helps to form and direct the larger society, so too is the
Church a reflection of that same society. If society as a whole is in denial about
the reality of childhood sexual abuse, then so is the Church. Because of this,
adult survivors have by default become an invisible, lost, non-population. Only
recently has the subject of childhood abuse become an issue addressed in
seminary training or pastoral counseling courses. In addition, the very nature of
the Church makes it an ideal hunting ground for certain pedophiles: there is a
ready-made population of victims since many members are married and have
children. These children are generally taught by their parents, and by the
Church, to hold their leaders in high regard, and to give them complete and total

trust in all things at all times. If abuse becomes public, there may be a tendency to discount the event, or deny it ever happened. There may be present the attitude which places equal blame upon the victim who may be ostracized, shunned, or even asked to leave the Church.

Another source of confusion can be traced to the conflict between the positions of religious indoctrination and spiritual education in childhood. By spiritual education I mean an underlying attitude on the part of the child's parents, and the educators in his Church, of drawing out from that child his own unique formulations of a Higher Power (as he understands Him) and strengthening this relationship between that child and his Higher Power. Each child is encouraged to investigate many paths, explore alternative imageries, and asked when mature to then define for himself this most private of all relationships. In such a healthy atmosphere there is little or no discrepancy between a child's "gut god" (which is based upon experience) and his intellectual or "head god" (based upon education).[1]

The opposite of this, religious indoctrination, is a position which strictly and rigidly defines for that child how he should, or should not, relate to his Higher Power. With this mentality, some adults' totalitarian definition of a Higher Power is autocratically preserved even at the expense of a child's personal experience. Extreme examples of this position are having been raised in a home characterized by religious fanaticism, or having experienced sexual abuse associated with religious or satanic ritual. In such pathological situations the results are the same: the creation of an overwhelming gap between a survivor's "gut god" and his "head god" along with the gross distortion, if not the complete destruction, of a child's relationship with his Higher Power. According to Father Loegering, the following is a list of frightening "gut god" images, in which adult survivors commonly see their Higher Power as:

- a mean, unjust, critical, or strict judge often seen sitting on a throne.
- very far away or distant.
- dead.
- a dirty old man.
- naked and hanging on the cross.
- naked and hanging on the cross with an erect penis.
- an old or young man with a knife.
- an old or young man with a stick or club.
- a sculptured bust of God (often visible only from the waist or shoulders up).
- a darkness or an impenetrable void.
- ANGRY (and in combination with any of the above).[2]

With the above list in mind, it is easy to see why some adult survivors simply cannot employ the more traditional Christian images of a Higher Power (i.e., The Prophet, The Bridegroom, The Crucified, The Resurrected, etc.).

Father Loegering notes, "When adult survivors are still comfortable enough to dare allow their Higher Power an image involving the human body, there are some consistent themes which follow specific patterns."[3] If the perpetrator had been an older male, many survivors image their Higher Power as the youthful Christ, but may find the idea of God as an older male figure very disturbing. If the perpetrator had been a younger male, many survivors are able to picture their Higher Power as Father, but are unable or unwilling to picture a younger Jesus figure. In those cases where the image of any masculine Higher Power is too threatening, the image of Mother is one feminine manifestation of Divine Being which is at least acceptable and familiar. If the perpetrator had been female, survivors have similar difficulty with benevolent feminine imagery as their Higher Power.[4]

Often when adult survivors do report a more positive image of a Higher Power the descriptions are typically more abstract, impersonal, or unconventional.[3] The roots of this alternative perspective on a Higher Power may originate from an overall denial system developed by the survivor which blocks all associations with a Higher Power that has any physical body because of the trauma originally inflicted upon their own bodies. In his work with adult survivors, Father Loegering has found that some of the often reported, less frightening "gut god" images to be:

- a cloud.
- a mountain.
- a "life force."
- a soft or bright light.
- a triangle.
- an "Oho de Deos" (literally "Eye of God"; this is a common type of Christian folk art native to the Southwestern United States).
- a safe place or room without entries or exists.
- an open or empty field.[5]

Because of these highly disturbing "gut images" of a Higher Power, or those which are highly unconventional, an adult survivor will naturally feel a great deal of spiritual isolation. In some Churches there are very strict rules, either written or unwritten, about what will or will not be considered acceptable imageries of a Higher Power. For example, within most of western Protestantism, the traditional images of God are male (not female), while the sexual aspects of this male Higher Power are rarely fully acknowledged.[6] A survivor's innate sense of isolation is made all the more real if he attempts to talk about his own images and feelings only to have them discounted, ignored, belittled, or rejected outright. He may even be asked to leave the Church entirely because of them. This insensitivity to his spiritual crisis only reinforces his sense of loneliness, increases his guilt for having such thoughts in the first place, deepens his sense of shame, exaggerates his hopelessness, and invariably compounds, rather than clarifies, his confusion.[7] "Hopefully, if a survivor reaches out for spiritual guidance his needs will be taken seriously, or he will wisely be referred to someone who can assist him," is the advice offered by Father Loegering.

For survivors who have very negative "gut god" images of a Higher Power, Father Loegering offers several suggestions to follow in order to begin to reestablish a spiritual relationship with Him. First, give your adult self permission to accept whatever images of a Higher Power the little boy inside of you happens to have, even if they are frightening. As your adult self begins to accept your inner child's scary images they will become less frightening as you talk about them to someone who will listen. Your adult self will also begin to see how your inner child can quite naturally have such images of a Higher Power, especially if you can keep in mind that they originate from your having been abused in the first place.

> *"While the trauma of childhood sexual abuse has indeed damaged or destroyed your image of a God, realize that your God is Himself not destroyed by this evil.* **The distinction between our childhood** *perception* **of a God and the** *reality* **of our Higher Power in our adult lives needs to made strongly and clearly."[5]**

If you cannot find someone to talk to concerning your spiritual issues, then focus upon this problem within either your Daily Journal or your 12 Step Journal, or both. Within your Recovery Journals you can begin to dialogue with your inner child about his "gut image" of his Higher Power. Let the little boy inside of you openly and freely express his feelings. Let him have a "voice" which can give words and form to his frightening images. If you need to, give the little boy inside of you permission to yell at God within the pages of your Journals. Over the years I have done a lot of yelling at my Higher Power. I first began to do so within my Journals. Later on in my Recovery I started to literally yell at my Higher Power with my voice. So far I have not been blasted by lightning, swallowed by a tornado, squashed by an earthquake, or spontaneously set aflame.

If you, or others, have considered your particular images of a Higher Power unusual, keep in mind that you are probably not the only one who has ever used that particular image. Within his best selling books, *The Hero With A Thousand Faces* and *The Power of Myth*, Joseph Campbell explores the myriad ways in which the Higher Power has come to be known at different places, among numerous cultures, and over generations of time.[8] It is odd to realize that the Higher Power has frequently made Himself known in places other than your nearby church building. The Buddha earned his enlightenment while sitting beneath the Bo tree. Moses discovered his Higher Power in the Burning Bush which was not consumed by the flames. Throughout the ages the Higher Power has been met again and again in the dry depths of the desert, along the wind blown shore of the sea, beside the quiet pools and creeks of the forest, amidst the marketplace, and in the middle of back roads in all lands. The Higher Power has also been known by any number of now strange-sounding names, but to those who spoke them they were most familiar and intimate: Mother Earth, Brother or Sister Moon, Father Sun, The Lord of the Dance, The Light of Lights, The Ancient of Days, or That Which Is.

In the more contemplative and introspective traditions, one of the goals of spiritual pilgrimage is freeing the ego of false darkness and releasing the light-filled ego that is the true Self. Unfortunately, one of the primary effects for the adult survivor of sexual abuse is an apparent shattering of the ego. Because of sexual abuse, our perceptions of our divine nature became fragmented and confused. Our spiritual relationship with our Higher Power never was fully severed, though it seemed that way through the eye of our inner child. Underneath the many layers of fallen debris caused by the abuse we suffered as children, as well as the resulting complications throughout our adult lives, that primal relationship remained hidden much like a candle burning in the depths of a cave: ever present, but unseen.

Through Recovery, however, we begin to heal the damaged perceptions of our ego and liberate the eternal child which is within us all. As we follow our spiritual path seeking ever greater understandings of our Higher Power we will be able to challenge the confusion and darkness we know all too well. Eventually along the way we begin to know, and even experience, what Kahlil Gibran calls our "god self."[9] At the very beginning of our Recovery, it may be confusing for our minds to know what to do to help heal the heart of our inner child. Thus, the following Exercises have been included. After the Exercises for Step Two is a collection of model prayers for you to consider using throughout the remaining Steps of Recovery.

> **"Come to the cliff," He said.**
> **They said, "We are afraid."**
> **"Come to the cliff," He said.**
> **They came.**
> **He pushed them.**
> **And they flew.**
> **— *Saying from the Shamans***

12 Step Journal Exercises for
Step Two

1. How would you rate your family's attitude about religion on the following scales? You can simply mark the spot on the scale that you think is correct. You can also mark only those scales you think apply to your family.

Closed Minded	1 5 10	Open Minded
Totalitarian	1 5 10	Progressive
Ask No Questions	1 5 10	Questioning OK
Intolerant of Others	1 5 10	Tolerant of Others
Unhealthy	1 5 10	Healthy
Fearful	1 5 10	Loving
Strict	1 5 10	Permissive

2. Did anyone in your family ever use religion as a means of maintaining control over you or other family members?

   Yes ___ No ___ Uncertain ___

If yes, who were those people?

  A. _____

  B. _____

3. Was the sexual abuse you experienced associated with any church function or religious ceremony?

   Yes ___ No ___

If yes, what were these functions or ceremonies?

  A. _____

  B. _____

4. Was the person who abused you associated with any church or religious denomination?

   Yes ___ No ___ Uncertain ___

If yes, what were those churches or denominations?

  A. _____

  B. _____

5. If you were abused by a person associated with a church or denomination what was that person's position?

___ priest or pastor   ___ Sunday school teacher

___ choir leader   ___ music director

___ church camp counselor   ___ lay worker

___ Other   A. _____

              B. _____

6. If you are able to do so, try to write out below the "head god" image that was taught to you as a child. This image is usually the traditional picture or pictures of a Higher Power that were acceptable to the Church in which you were raised.

7. The following is a list of frightening "gut god" images which adult survivors commonly report. Do any of the following apply to your "gut god" image of a Higher Power?*

___ a mean, unjust, critical, or strict judge often seen sitting on a throne.

___ very far away or distant.

___ dead.

___ a dirty old man.

___ naked and hanging of the cross.

___ naked and hanging on the cross with an erect penis.

___ an old or young man with a knife.

___ an old or young man with a stick or club.

___ a sculptured bust of God (often visible only from the waist or shoulders up).

___ a darkness or an impenetrable void.

___ ANGRY (and in combination with any of the above).

___ Other frightening "gut god" images

    A. _____

    B. _____

8. The following are some of the less frightening "gut god" images of a Higher Power that some might consider unconventional. Which of these applies to your "gut god" image of a Higher Power?*

    ___ a cloud.

    ___ a mountain.

    ___ a "life force."

    ___ a soft or bright light.

    ___ a triangle.

    ___ a safe place or room without entries or exists.

    ___ an open or empty field.

    ___ an "Oho de Deos."

    ___ Other unconventional images of a Higher Power

        A. _____

        B. _____

9. If your "gut god" image is upsetting or frightening, is there an alternative image that you can picture or create with your mind's eye? Even unconventional imagery is acceptable. _____

_____

_____

_____

_____

_____

10. What is the "gut self" image that your inner wounded child has of himself?

_____

_____

_____

_____

_____

_____

11. If you are able to do so, how would you describe the relationship between your "gut god" and your "gut self" images? Is it safe or threatening? Scary or frightening? Where are these two images in relationship to each other? Take some time and try to give this answer as much visual detail as you can.*

_____
_____
_____
_____
_____
_____

12. If the above imagery was uncomfortable to you, what things could you change in the imagery that could make it safer for your "gut self" to communicate with your "gut god"? These changes in the imagery do not have to be logical or make sense rationally. They can be as fanciful and as magical as you wish them to be. As these various changes or ideas come to mind over time, please feel free to come back and rewrite this section of your 12 Step Recovery Journal.*_____

_____
_____
_____
_____
_____

13. When you have been able to create an image of your "gut god" and your "gut self" in a relationship, even if this relationship makes no sense to anyone but you, what would be the things that they would say to each other? You might wish to write out the beginning portion of this conversation below. If you feel the need to do so, you might consider continuing this dialogue under the heading "Dialogue with my Higher Power" in your Recovery Journal as your healing evolves.*

_____
_____
_____
_____
_____
_____

Note: "*" indicates questions based upon Father Loegering's material.

44

Prayers for Recovery

The following prayers for Recovery have been written within the context of the Christian tradition. Throughout the ages men have come to know their Higher Power by any number of names: God, Allah, Mother Earth, Yahweh, The Great the Spirit, The Absolute, He Who Is, Brahman, as well as others. Please feel free to adapt these prayers to your own particular spiritual path as you work out your Recovery through the use of the 12 Steps.

Lord, just as you told the mourning family of Lazarus, "He still lives, yet, is but asleep," help me to know my wounded inner child has not died, but is still alive within me although asleep.

Lord, as you were raised from the dead, allow me to find New Life this day through you.

Lord, let your Spirit intercede for me, for I have no words. My soul longs for your presence.

Lord, bless my inner child who is in pain. Remember him to your Father.

———◆———

Lord, help me to remember your words, "Whatsoever is done even to the least of these is also done to me." Help me to realize inasmuch as I was sexually abused, so too were you abused. Help me to know when I am most alone, you are with me.

———◆———

Father, help me to be thanks-filled this day as I rediscover the miracle of The Resurrection.

Father, help me to remember your first miracle at the wedding feast. Just as water can be changed to wine, help me to know my pains and sorrows can likewise be transfigured into joy and laughter.

◆

Father, you have already fulfilled your promise of New Life. Help me to let go of my own plans and designs. Allow me to know your Will this day.

◆

Lord, at times feelings of helplessness and power-lessness overwhelm me on my path towards Recovery. Help me to remember you also once felt abandoned by your Father as when you cried out on The Tree the words, "My God, my God, why have you forsaken me?"

◆

Lord, my spirit is troubled and my mind is confused. Grant me the gifts of inner silence, clarity, and peace.

◆

Father, the nights seem so very long. My dreams are filled with terror. Protect me with your Grace, and lighten the darkness with your Love.

◆

Father, my days are often filled with visions from the past. Remind me of how yesterday is only yesterday, and today is but today.

◆

Lord, you have called me to be born again this day in spirit. Help me to let go of the past.

◆

Lord, grant me the Serenity to accept the fact I cannot change my having been sexually abused as a child, the Courage to break free from the bonds of revictimization, and the Wisdom to know how to do so.

*Lord, all good gifts come from you. Help me to redis-
cover the joys of your gifts of masculinity, sexuality,
intimacy, and love. Help me to reclaim my forgotten
gentleness, strength, and power.*

◆

*Lord, forgive me those things which I have done to
others because I was once wounded. Grant me the
Strength and the Courage to mend those hurts I have
caused.*

◆

*Father, forgive me my own shortcomings caused by my
denial. Help me to see clearly the wounded child within
myself. Show my inner parent the paths I must take to
heal him.*

◆

*Lord, in the past I have turned to drugs and alcohol to
kill my inner child's pain. I ask your forgiveness in
harming myself this way. Help me to turn to you, for you
are the source of the waters which quench true thirst.*

◆

*Lord, bless those who guide me in my Recovery. May
they be open to your gifts of learning, wisdom, honesty,
and compassion.*

Step 3

$\blacklozenge$

Awareness

We become aware of how this abuse has had a powerful influence upon our lives and how it has controlled us.

The Six Life areas, which were explored earlier, are used throughout this chapter to help organize and identify the influences that sexual abuse has had upon our lives. In reading these pages you may find yourself experiencing any number of intense emotions. If this happens to you, do not feel that you have to keep on reading. You have permission to stop at any point. Close the book and take a deep breath. Go for a long walk. Grab the tissues and cry. Get angry. Slam a door. Give yourself time to calm down and collect your thoughts. If you need to, talk to members of your Recovery Team who can help you through this time. You are not alone in these struggles.

Keep in mind that there is nothing wrong with feeling swamped by jumbled memories or confused impressions. You may experience physical reactions such as nausea, constipation, or dizziness. **You are having normal reactions. The sexual abuse you experienced was, and is, wrong. The feelings you have in response to that abuse are not wrong.** While the hard work of grieving is never easy, it is something which you can go through without dying (although you may not necessarily feel that way). Whatever you do, do nothing which harms yourself or others. Do not take your pain out on others. Do not drink and drive. Do not cut or mutilate yourself. Do not kill yourself. Try to be aware of those things which have not been helpful in the past.

The point of this chapter is not to make you feel hopeless or powerless. What you know can free you. If you are able to recognize revictimization in the Social Life Area, you will be more able to recognize this pattern in the other areas of your life. Healing feeds into more healing, and Recovery can begin to take on an energy and flow of its own.

If we cannot directly solve a problem in one Life Area, we might be able to address that problem indirectly by focusing upon our strengths and talents in the other Life Areas. Thus, it is very important that we first become aware of these positive aspects in our lives which can empower and enable us to continue our Recovery. Rather than allow ourselves to become entangled by what we **cannot** do, we focus upon those things which we **can** do, and can change. It is possible that the difficulty which overwhelmed us will be resolved entirely or reduced to manageable proportions. You already have successful survival strategies, although you may not recognize them. The very fact that you are alive proves you have been doing something right. It is extremely important that we become aware of these assets as we rebuild our lives. It makes little sense to arrive at a construction site where we are remodeling a damaged house only to forget to bring our tools. For this reason an inventory entitled "My Positive Attributes, Resources, and Strengths" has been included at the beginning of this chapter. If you can recognize one positive element, seek it out and nurture it.

Instead of using check lists or rating scales, I suggest a different format for Step 3 exercises. If there is a particular topic or paragraph within this Step which describes how childhood abuse has negatively influenced your adult life, please write this out on the exercise pages which follow.

During this stage our attention spans are often very short and we can easily become mentally and emotionally overloaded. **You do not have to become aware of all the negative effects of childhood sexual abuse in order for you to continue with your Recovery**. You have permission to work this Step as many times as you need to. Coming back to this Step at some future point is not an indication that you failed in your first efforts. Returning to this Step is a sign that your healing is continuing to deepen. So, try to set your own speed and work this Step only as long as you wish before moving on.

> **He that will not apply new remedies**
> **must expect new evils.**
> — *Bacon*

My Positive Attributes, Resources, and Strengths in the Psychological Life Area

Which of the following words describe some of your positive mental and emotional attributes?

___ stubborn   ___ courageous
___ strong-willed   ___ careful
___ thoughtful   ___ creative
___ kind   ___ sympathetic
___ compassionate   ___ considerate
___ resilient   ___ gutsy
___ artistic   ___ intuitive
___ flexible   ___ soft-hearted
___ methodical   ___ organized
___ normal intelligence
___ Other mental and emotional attributes

A. _____

B. _____

Which of the following do you feel are your mental and emotional resources?

___ I have learned to survive.
___ I have a supportive therapist.
___ I have a mind that still thinks.
___ I have a heart that still feels.
___ Other psychological resources

A. _____

B. _____

Which of the following do you feel are your mental and emotional strengths?

___ I am beginning to challenge hopelessness.
___ I am beginning to challenge helplessness.
___ I am beginning to challenge powerlessness.
___ I am learning how to listen to my feelings.
___ I am learning how to listen to my thoughts.
___ I am learning how to listen to my intuition.
___ I am learning how to change.
___ I am learning how to work with my grief.
___ I am learning that I do have emotional and mental gifts and talents.
___ Other mental and emotional strengths

A. _____

B. _____

My Positive Attributes, Resources, and Strengths in the Spiritual Life Area

Which of the following words describe some of your positive spiritual attributes?

___ open-minded	___ dedicated
___ earnest	___ sincere
___ serious	___ curious
___ committed	___ devout
___ wholehearted	___ genuine
___ determined	___ resolute
___ authentic	___ steadfast
___ faithful	___ questioning
___ unpretentious	___ temperate

___ Other spiritual attributes

A. _____

B. _____

Which of the following do you feel are your spiritual resources?

___ I have a spiritual tradition to rely upon.

___ I have a spiritual advisor who helps me.

___ I have people in my life who will pray for me.

___ I have a Higher Power.

___ I have an inner Self which cannot die.

___ Other spiritual resources

A. _____

B. _____

Which of the following do you feel are your spiritual strengths?

___ I have enough faith to continue living.

___ I have enough wisdom to continue to seek out my Higher Power.

___ I have enough hope to continue my spiritual quest.

___ I am learning to trust my Higher Power.

___ I am learning to follow my heart.

___ I am learning to live out of my true gifts and talents.

___ I am learning that I do have spiritual strengths.

___ Other spiritual strengths

A. _____

B. _____

My Positive Attributes, Resources, and Strengths in the Sexual Life Area

Which of the following words describe some of your positive sexual attributes?

___ empathetic   ___ sensitive
___ intimate   ___ tender
___ sensual   ___ affectionate
___ trustworthy   ___ faithful
___ caring   ___ romantic
___ compassionate   ___ loving
___ strong   ___ playful
___ earthy   ___ passionate
___ erotic   ___ responsible
___ masculine   ___ knowledgeable
___ Other sexual attributes

A. _____

B. _____

Which of the following do you feel are your sexual resources?

___ I have a partner, lover or spouse who helps me.
___ I have books which help me learn about sexuality.
___ I have a Recovery Team Member with whom I can talk about my sexual concerns.
___ I have a body which is sexually responsive.
___ I have a mind which can appreciate sensuality.
___ I have a heart which can share both my joys and fears concerning my sexuality.
___ Other sexual resources

A. _____

B. _____

Which of the following do you feel are your sexual strengths?

___ I am beginning to rediscover my sexuality.
___ I am learning to be gentle with myself sexually.
___ I am learning that I have the right to say "No" when I need to say "No" to sexual requests or demands.
___ I am beginning to say "No" in these situations.
___ I am learning that I have the right to say "Yes" when I want to say "Yes" to my own and my partner's sexual wants.
___ I am beginning to say "Yes" in these situations.

___ I am learning safer sex techniques.

___ I am beginning to practice safer sex techniques.

___ I am learning to relax when thinking or talking about sexual issues.

___ Other sexual strengths

A. _____

B. _____

My Positive Attributes, Resources, and Strengths in the Physical Life Area

Which of the following words describe some of your positive physical attributes?

___ can hear   ___ can see
___ can smell   ___ can touch
___ can taste   ___ can walk
___ can run   ___ can swim
___ can talk   ___ can exercise
___ in fair health   ___ in good health
___ clean   ___ neat
___ well-groomed
___ Other physical attributes

A. _____
B. _____

Which of the following do you feel are your physical resources?

___ I have a decent and safe place to live.
___ I have a body that works.
___ I know how to care for my body.
___ I know how to shop for healthy foods.
___ I know how to cook good meals.
___ I have a Recovery Team member who will help me with my physical problems or rehabilitation.
___ I have a Recovery Team member who will help me with my chemical addictions.
___ Other physical resources

A. _____
B. _____

Which of the following do you feel are your physical strengths?

___ I am learning to listen to my body.
___ I am learning to take better care of my health.
___ I am learning to trust my senses.
___ I am learning to trust my gut-level instincts and intuitions.
___ I am beginning to be gentle with my body.
___ I am beginning to eat good food.
___ I am beginning to gain the weight I need to gain.
___ I am beginning to lose the weight I need to lose.
___ I am in Recovery for my chemical and drug dependencies.
___ I am beginning to think about my use of drugs and alcohol.

____ I am learning to work with my pain.

____ Other physical strengths

A. _____

B. _____

My Positive Attributes, Resources, and Strengths in the Social Life Area

Which of the following words describe some of your positive social attributes?

___ loyal	___ observant
___ reliable	___ honest
___ tolerant	___ patient
___ non-judging	___ dependable
___ authentic	___ trustworthy
___ stable	___ genuine
___ straightforward	___ ethical
___ conscientious	___ tolerant
___ gentle	___ street-wise
___ sensitive	___ outgoing
___ Other social attributes	

A. _____

B. _____

Which of the following do you feel are your social resources?

___ I have friend/s who support my Recovery.

___ I have family member/s who support my Recovery.

___ I attend a Recovery Support group.

___ I have a schedule which helps me organize my time.

___ I have a schedule which helps me set healthy boundaries.

___ Other social resources

A. _____

B. _____

Which of the following do you feel are your social strengths?

___ I am learning to face my irrational fear of people, places and things.

___ I am learning that I have the right to live in safe and decent housing.

___ I am learning that I am a good friend to others.

___ I am learning that I have the right to surround myself with supportive, loving people.

___ I am learning to reach out for help.

___ I am a good friend to others.

___ Other social strengths

A. _____

B. _____

My Positive Attributes, Resources, and Strengths in the Economic Life Area

Which of the following words describe some of your positive financial and occupational attributes?

___ hard-working	___ respected
___ disciplined	___ educated
___ skilled	___ flexible
___ sensible	___ careful
___ meticulous	___ dependable
___ prudent	___ creative
___ effective	___ professional
___ dedicated	___ thrifty
___ moderate	___ resourceful

___ Other financial and occupational attributes

A. _____

B. _____

Which of the following do you feel are your financial and occupational resources?

___ I have a job and an income.

___ I receive a retirement check.

___ I receive a disability income.

___ I have an accountant on my Recovery Team.

___ I have a financial advisor on my Recovery Team.

___ I have a savings account.

___ I have a retirement account.

___ Other economic resources

A. _____

B. _____

Which of the following do you feel are your financial and occupational strengths?

___ I am a good employee.

___ I have some occupational training.

___ I have started back to school for more education or additional job training.

___ I have a high school diploma or the equivalent.

___ I have a college degree.

___ I budget my time.

___ I budget my money.

___ I am working on a savings account.

___ I am working on a retirement account.

___Other economic strengths

A. _____

B. _____

The Psychological Life Area

The psychological destruction resulting from childhood sexual abuse can be compared to the results of plugging a partially assembled computer into a thousand volt power line, and then flipping the "On" switch. The basic neurological wiring of any child is simply not designed to handle, in a normal fashion, this traumatic overload. Somewhere a circuit-breaker has to automatically trip in order to keep the entire system from frying; denial is the primary mechanism for self-protection. However, denial is a rather complex defensive system with at least three major variations: **repression, suppression,** and **dissociation.** All of these may be involved in protecting the self from the abuse, but typically one of them becomes the dominant coping pattern.

In the case of **repression** all memories of the abuse are blocked from conscious awareness. As far as the victim is concerned, the sexual assaults simply never happened. If you ask an adult who used repression to survive their childhood, they may talk about how wonderful their childhood was, or remember their past in glowing, idyllic terms. What they tell you about their growing-up years sounds too good to be true.

When **supression** is the dominant defense mechanism, the person will acknowledge the abuse, but will omit the emotional and psychological pain. A characteristic of suppression is the lack of emotion, even when describing the most horrific abuses. Such a person may tell you how he was molested at age 11, but sees it as something which was either good for him, or quite enjoyable. It is not uncommon for this person to view this as the first time he ever became aware of his hetero-, homo-, or bi-sexuality.

In the case of **dissociation,** survivors often describe the perception that, at the time of the abuse, their sense of self, or consciousness, left their bodies. As the assault continues it is as if they were watching the scene happening to someone else from outside themselves. The abuse happens, but, in essence, not to them. Often they may simply "check out" and be there in body, but their minds are literally someplace else. Later in life this psychological survival technique may result in the still much-debated formation of multiple personalities.

While all of these defensive strategies may make little sense to someone on the outside, on some level denial was chosen by the child simply because it was the absolute best he could do with what little resources he had available to him at the time! Blaming the child within for using any or all of these coping strategies is simply another form of victimization! If the truth about the abuse is revealed when a child is first sexually assaulted, and he receives professional treatment along with the rest of his family, the life-long effects of these defense mechanisms can be reduced. If they are not addressed, the little boy may grow up to be an adult who is confused, forgetful, fragmented, depressed, passive, scared, angry, or even someone he literally does not know.

If the facts are not discovered shortly after the molestation, the intense feelings associated with the trauma will remain buried, long-forgotten within the child's mind. However, no defense mechanism makes the past go away forever. These devices just block the pain from conscious awareness. Such a situation is much like the mythological box into which Prometheus once drove all of the evils of the world, but which Pandora later re-opened. No matter how tight the lid on any "Pandora's Box" of hidden secrets, the effects of the abuse will eventually begin to leak out in the form of numerous and primary symptoms. And until Recovery begins, these symptoms will be present in some form or fashion for an entire lifetime! This psychological short-circuiting, and the subsequent symptoms which follow, can most accurately be diagnosed clinically as Post-Traumatic Stress Disorder.[1]

Due to unconscious associations between the environment in which we were abused, and people, places and things now present in our adult lives, what appear to be normal circumstances to others may produce high levels of anxiety, fear, anger, paranoia and/or panic in us. However, due to our over-riding denial, we adult survivors will have no idea why this multitude of common, everyday situations causes such powerful, and painful, responses. Others may ridicule, discount, or criticize our mysterious feelings. They may even laugh at us because of our eccentric behaviors.

Examples of stimuli which produce these reactions may include being alone in a room with another person, or being touched by others. Sexual excitement or activity, including masturbation, also may be frightening and upsetting. Interpersonal relationships involving power, conflict, or even the possibility of conflict, may trigger high levels of anxiety. Rooms, houses, or locations similar to where the abuse occurred induce fear responses as well.

Another source of discomfort are individuals who physically or be-haviorally resemble the one who committed the abuse. Even people with the same name as the abuser may produce unsettling responses. The time of day, or season, can also trigger these reactions. The most sadistic sexual abuse I suffered was in the fall of the year and I still find myself getting anxious whenever I realize the leaves are changing and the weather is becoming cooler and more windy. Depending upon an individual's specific history, they may be highly upset by violent television shows, horror movies, nudity in the presence of others, certain types of smells; the list goes on.

However, of all the psychological scars from childhood carried by adult survivors, the two most insidious are an overwhelming sense of hopelessness, and powerful feelings of apathy about the future. Read that last sentence again. It is important that you fully understand this fact.

As time passes, the number of symptoms will continue to grow as the three forms of denial fail more often and more intensely. This is true since repression and suppression, as well as dissociation, are not self-limiting survival skills. Eventually these coping strategies become the dominant pattern by which all life difficulties are managed. As these defensive strategies continue to operate by blocking unpleasant adult realities, new truths which are painful and need to be heard are also ignored. These layers of complications, known as secondary problems within this text, eventually have a profound influence upon all of the six Life Areas in our adult lives. One example of such secondary problem is chemical dependency. It is not uncommon for adult survivors to develop drug and alcohol problems as they try to cope with complications arising from the chronic pain of repressed trauma. Any Pandora's Box can only hold so much, and under enough pressure even the best of containment vessels will fracture.

Considering the high number of symptoms adult male survivors typically present (sexual disorders, depression, major mental illnesses, anxiety, paranoia, sleep disturbances, substance abuse, personality disorders, etc.), it is very easy to overlook the underlying core issue of childhood sexual abuse and thus, misdiagnose these difficulties or symptoms. Until these many problems are recognized as indicators of a deeper issue, an adult survivor may spend the rest of his life desperately searching for cures. Unfortunately, such therapeutic treatments will simply become a means of managing the symptoms. Inevitably the old difficulties, or even new ones, will resurface if the psychological wounds remain untreated. Such symptoms, or leaks in the box, can be the clues which to lead to Recovery, provided they are recognized for what they are. When the symptoms are diagnosed correctly, and the adult survivor takes the first of the 12 Steps, active Recovery can begin.

How Childhood Sexual Abuse Has Influenced My Psychological Life Area

Psychological Problems_____

_____

_____

_____

_____

_____

_____

If you cannot think of a way to work on this issue directly, is there another Life Area which may help you cope with this problem indirectly?

        Yes ___ No ___ Uncertain ___

If yes, what other Life Area might you use? How could this Life Area help you cope with this other problem?

Life Area _____

How _____

_____

_____

The person on my Recovery Team who might help me with this problem is

_____

The Spiritual Life Area

Anyone who has ever lived or worked with children knows they often develop the strangest notions when it comes to picturing a Supreme Being. Hopefully, as they mature, so does their understanding of a Higher Power. Through proper training and guidance a child develops his image of a Higher Power in his own way, and at his own level of understanding, as spiritual needs can only be met in a spiritual manner. There are no substitutions.

Adult survivors often thirst spiritually, but continue to remain unfulfilled. As was pointed out in the previous chapter, the relationship with our Higher Power is the one most frequently and severely damaged. For us Men of the Wounded Child, there remains within us the little boy who experienced being abandoned by our mother and father, family and friends, and who still feels forever abandoned by his Higher Power. Nevertheless, there remain those spiritual needs only a relationship with our Higher Power can satisfy.

About the time I began keeping a journal I also started to question my own spirituality. While my upbringing was within the Protestant tradition, I now found myself exploring other religious perspectives. This openness, I suspect, came from my family's varied background and from the fact I lived in many states and the Orient while my father was in the United States Air Force. Being brought up in an environment where differences are the norm and respected, I found it easy to move past the confines of my own tradition. Somewhere I hoped I would find a place where my spirit would finally feel at home.

As this pilgrimage continued I discovered myself attracted to many of the Western monastic traditions. Ultimately, I began making private retreats to various guest houses supported by the monasteries of the Cistertian Order, or the Trappists. In these places I found something inherently comforting about the daily rhythm of prayer, work, and praise. I saw in the monks' gentle, contemplative approach to meditation something I longed to experience for myself. While walking the fields at midday or sitting quietly in the chapel during early morning Vigils, I most truly felt at one with my Higher Power. At these sanctuaries supported by the Brothers there is one basic request made of retreatants: that all guests respect the collective silence and be mindful of the daily schedule. Beyond this simple rule, there are no other requirements. If you need to sleep, then sleep. If you wish to attend all, or none of the daily services, then this is acceptable as well. The attitude of the Brothers can best be summed up by the statement, "We offer a structure for your time if you choose to use it. We also offer a place for you to rest, and food to eat. Beyond this, we will not interfere. What you need to do here is between you and God."

At first, I always experienced a mixture of conflicting impulses concerning these retreats. A part of me knew this was exactly what I needed to be doing, while another part was always deeply disturbed by the silence. Even in this, the most accepting and safe place, I would often wake up in the middle of the night with horrific nightmares, or I could not sleep at all. Sometimes late at night I would feel overwhelming paranoia for no reason. After a while I simply accepted the fact it was normal for me to be up all night and to sleep during the day. During one retreat this inner turmoil was so strong I packed my bags at midnight and left the next morning immediately after breakfast. Something was gnawing at my guts, and it scared me. Occasionally I toyed with the idea I must in some way be possessed, or worse, cursed by God. How else could I explain the incessant urge within to seek out a contemplative lifestyle, and at the very same time experience other equally powerful urges which pulled me back into the secular world of day-to-day crises, chaos, turmoil and confusion.

During this time I intensely explored Eastern meditation techniques, hoping they might grant me the inner peace I sought. However, no matter what technique I used to quiet myself, I could never reach the level of physical relaxation necessary for truly open contemplation. My mind rarely settled down no matter how much time I took. In those instances when I was finally able to relax through the use of deep breathing exercises, I would occasionally find myself flooded with overwhelming dread. This sensation of impending doom would become so intense that I would literally come out of my sitting position in the middle of a panic attack! At times the meditations would bring some peace, for which I was thankful. Other times, they would only bring terror. How could something which was supposed to offer tranquility bring nothing but pandemonium?

I now recognize the source of the many barriers I was experiencing. The difficulty I had in sleeping while on retreat came from a basic unresolved fear of being in an unfamiliar place surrounded by unknown males. I stayed up all night simply because I did not feel safe. My lack of serenity during meditation came from the chronic hypervigilance associated with Post-Traumatic Stress Disorder. I had unconsciously adapted to living in a constant state of panic. Relaxing to a more normal level of stress felt threatening, and I might lose control (and if I lost control I might be raped again).

The fear of possession I once felt had some sense of truth to it, although not so much in the literal sense (by a demon), but rather by the wounded child within me. It was not my adult self who once wished to drive the nails into the hands of The Christ on Good Friday, but rather the enraged child who still felt abandoned by his Higher Power.

Somehow, we must find some way of forgiving our Higher Power for not fulfilling our childlike expectation that He is all-powerful. He is not. Our Higher Power can not re-write the past. However, this Higher Power is all-powerful in the sense He can help us change the present, and in doing so re-write our future. The spiritual home we seek is not one outside ourselves, but rather a place within at the very depths of our being, the cave of the heart, where only we and our Higher Power can meet, and commune as one.

How Childhood Sexual Abuse Has Influenced My Spiritual Life Area

Spiritual Problems _____ _

_____

_____

_____

_____

_____

_____

If you cannot think of a way to work on this issue directly, is there another Life Area which may help you cope with this problem indirectly?

        Yes ___ No ___ Uncertain ___

If yes, what other Life Area might you use? How could this Life Area help you cope with this other problem?

Life Area _____ _

How _____

_____

_____

The person on my Recovery Team who might help me with this problem is

_____

The Sexual Life Area

Like our spiritual identity, our sexuality is a fundamental issue. While it is obvious that sexual abuse in childhood seriously impairs adult sexual behavior, the mechanisms remain unclear. However, I would like to offer a hypothetical model which may explain dynamics through which this impairment occurs.

One of our most basic physiological reactions as human beings is the "fight-or-flight" response. When a person is under threat of physical harm the entire body instinctively responds in order to prepare the individual to either fight for his life, or to run for his life. In such threatening situations that part of the brain which is beyond our conscious control triggers the following biochemical changes: heartbeat rises dramatically; adrenalin levels skyrocket; mental attention becomes narrowly focused; muscles tense in preparation to act; respiration rates increase; and the digestive system shuts down. It is from these biological reactions the emotions of both anger and fear arise. For example, if someone is angry, they are often scared. Conversely, if someone is frightened, they can easily become enraged.

When a child is sexually abused this powerful fight-or-flight response is automatically activated. However, when this child is molested, he can neither run nor successfully fight back. On a fundamental behavioral level, sexual experience thus becomes associated with intense physical turmoil and extreme emotional upheaval. Even one such experience can lead to adverse associations between any sexual activity and the trauma of being sexually assaulted. In cases of repeated abuse these negative associations become even stronger, and can lead to crippling cases of learned helplessness involving all future sexual situations. When a child is sexually molested, love becomes hate, pleasure turns to pain, excitement is distorted into fear or rage, and intimacy is reduced to brutality.

If the abused child is sexually immature, at puberty he will have no experiential basis to judge the differences between normal and non-normal sexual responses. When this child's sexuality begins to emerge he will experience a great deal of agitation because of his past learning. It will be easy for him to erroneously assume the flood of intense, painful, and negative responses he feels are typical sexual reactions, especially if he has blocked all memories of having been abused.

As the child matures into adolescence the reproductive impulse for sexual experience becomes stronger and demands expression; at the same time there is the underlying negative behavioral conditioning which drives him away from sexual fulfillment. In fact, the sexual and the flight-or-fight responses are highly incompatible, as sexuality is most positively experienced when an individual is relaxed, calm, secure, and safe. Sexual desire cannot follow an expected course to full and pleasing orgasm if, at the same time, other parts of the body and brain are responding in panic.

Because of this past behavioral conditioning there may be high levels of tension (i.e., increased heart beat, accelerated adrenalin production, etc.) when a sexually developing abuse victim is around individuals of the same sex as the abuser. If the abuser was male, it is possible for the individual who was molested to assume this level of excitement indicates a homosexual orientation (if the victim was innately heterosexual), or that this is how sexual excitement is supposed to feel if the victim is homosexual. If the abuser was female, the abused male will have serious difficulties relating to women because of these conflicting response patterns. Such an approach-avoidance dilemma can only result in chronic maladaptive behavior until these underlying conflicts are addressed and treated. When the above issues are considered, it is clear how someone who was abused as a child can become confused and disturbed when he begins to reach sexual growth in adolescence. Indeed, the odds are rather high that such an individual would develop a number of serious sexual dysfunctions, especially if normal sexual issues or the realities of childhood sexual abuse are never discussed.

I think that these conflicting response patterns may also explain how some adult survivors develop compulsive sexual behaviors or disorders. While the child-victim may realize that he has no control at all **if** the sexual abuse happens, he may find some means of being able to control **how** or **when** it happens. By trial and error the sexually abused child may finally discover a means of pleasing his abuser and therefore develop those behaviors which minimize the pain inflicted upon him. The little boy inside figures out for himself that, "I might not be able to stop the abuse, but maybe I can at least keep it from hurting me so much."

These new-found sexual behaviors have the powerful, positive function of both decreasing his anxiety by giving him a little bit of control and decreasing the personal injury suffered. Later on an adult survivor may consciously or unconsciously act out sexually in a similar fashion whenever he is under stress, or finds himself in an intimate relationship. It is strangely ironic that an adult survivor's present compulsive sexual behavior may have had the past positive function of keeping him alive.

How Childhood Sexual Abuse Has Influenced My Sexual Life Area

Sexual problems_____

_____

_____

_____

_____

_____

_____

If you cannot think of a way to work on this issue directly, is there another Life Area which may help you cope with this problem indirectly?

Yes ___ No ___ Uncertain ___

If yes, what other Life Area might you use? How could this Life Area help you cope with this other problem?

Life Area _____

How _____

_____

_____

The person on my Recovery Team who might help me with this problem is

_____

The Physical Life Area

In addition to the expected problems caused by Post-Traumatic Stress Disorder, such as sleep disturbances and chronically high levels of anxiety, there are a number of other secondary physical complications which arise in adulthood. While the mind may be successful in consciously blocking the emotional trauma of abuse, the body still experiences, expresses, and remembers the effects of the abuse. Recovery also means physical healing.

We all, at one time or another, have had what is commonly known as a tension headache, caused by the stress in our bodies becoming localized, or centered, in the muscles of our shoulders or neck. We are aware only of the relentless pounding in our heads, often not realizing the stress we are under. Only when we have finally begun to be mindful of what this headache is trying to tell us about our lives, can we start to deal with the problem, and not simply eliminate the symptoms by taking a couple of aspirin.

This same basic process of our headaches' sending us signals is a much smaller, scaled-down version of more profound physical complications experienced by adult survivors. Like most persons under extreme conditions, chronic physical complications and the particular manner in which they are expressed is dependent upon which organ systems are vulnerable to attack due to the interplay of genetics and environment.[2] Such physical complications include high blood pressure, chronic cardiac problems, migraines, constipation, muscular disorders, chronic obesity, bulimia, or ulcers. However, for men of the wounded child the sources of their stress are insidious and more difficult to identify due to the effects of repression, suppression, and dissociation, and their pains much more extreme. If you forgot you were stuck this morning on the freeway for two and a half hours in the worst case of traffic grid-lock you ever saw, how could you possibly connect that incident with a splitting headache you suffer in the middle of the afternoon?

As a result of chronic discomfort caused by hypervigilance, an adult survivor may develop a dependency upon alcohol or tranquilizers in order to alleviate the anxiety he always experiences. If this ineffectual coping pattern continues unchallenged, true chemical addictions will only complicate an already messy situation. This survivor may also discover himself developing other chemical, or even behavioral, addictions to help him manage simultaneous problems with depression. The group of chemical dependencies includes caffeine, nicotine, amphetamines and pain-killers. Behavioral addictions include eating disorders, sexual addictions or even becoming a workaholic.

Not until my therapist, Betty, confronted me with my own self-destructive patterns did I realize how profoundly these physical complications influenced my own health. In the evenings I would drink, often to the point of passing out, just so I could sleep without having nightmares. The next morning I would consume far too much coffee to recover from this self-administered, drug-induced coma. I always seemed to have a cigarette in my hand to calm me down.

As a teenager and young adult I tended to go on eating binges. I always wondered why my weight had been a chronic problem. Now I understood: being fat was my unconscious attempt to make myself unattractive to Samuel, thus, keeping myself safe. The backlash of this strategy, however, was painful when my sixth grade classmates nicknamed me "Hippo." By then I already tipped the scales at an even two hundred and fifteen pounds, and was barely five foot one. The very same body armor which kept me safe also isolated me from others. Fortunately, Betty was wise enough to know while my emotional problems still needed to be handled in our therapy sessions together, my physical problems required a different, more direct approach. At this point she referred me to an associate who had been trained in body and massage therapy. When she first suggested this, my reactions were intensely negative: I simply did not want another strange male touching me. However, as I thought it over during the following weeks I realized she was right.

Any discussion of the physical complications of childhood sexual abuse would be incomplete if the topic of AIDS were not addressed. I am convinced that childhood sexual abuse has a role in the spread of AIDS. An adult male survivor who has not yet entered Recovery typically experiences a very conflicted sexual identity. If this person engages in unsafe sexual behaviors, he is automatically at risk for acquiring, and transmitting, AIDS. If he re-enacts his original victimization by participating in high-risk sexual activities such as unprotected anal intercourse with multiple partners, he only places himself, and others, in even greater jeopardy. Add to this a pervasive sense of hopelessness for the future, plus an impaired auto-immune system due to the long-term effects of PTSD or drug abuse (not to mention intravenous needle swapping), and you have a certain prescription for disaster.

How Childhood Sexual Abuse Has Influenced My Physical Life Area

Physical problems_____

_____

_____

_____

_____

_____

_____

If you cannot think of a way to work on this issue directly, is there another Life Area which may help you cope with this problem indirectly?

Yes ___ No ___ Uncertain ___

If yes, what other Life Area might you use? How could this Life Area help you cope with this other problem?

Life Area _____

How _____

_____

_____

The person on my Recovery Team who might help me with this problem is

_____

The Social Life Area

Two characteristics which separate us from other social species are the twin abilities to learn and to teach. There cannot be one without the other. We may either be unaware of this reality, or deny it, but we are all both students and teachers. It is with our parents in the context of our family of origin that we are first exposed to the obvious lessons of language, reading, and acceptable behavior. It is also here in the family unit that we absorb the more subtle instructions concerning hierarchies, roles, boundaries, sexuality, morality, and even self-image. As we mature through infancy and into childhood, we begin to interact with our extended families and to make our first tentative steps into the immediate social environments of school, church, neighborhood and community. During adolescence the number and range of teachers continues to expand as the tasks become more complex and challenging. As young adults we graduate from these provincial circles and begin to move into the larger, more independent, worlds of occupation or college. Eventually, as adults our horizons expand to include the establishment of our own families (as we choose to define them for ourselves), a career in life, national citizenship, and maybe even membership in the global community.

However, the natural progression which takes us full circle from youth, in which we are primarily the students, to adulthood, where we are then the teachers and caretakers for the next generation, is a circle which is extremely delicate, and ever so fragile. This continuity from generation to generation follows predictable patterns. An examination of this social cycle of life is most important to an understanding of how childhood sexual abuse affects not only the lives of its victims, but also the common well-being of humanity on the broadest levels.

In order to explore both the unique patterns of childhood, as well as the specific tasks of each stage, I will be using the developmental hypothesis offered by Erik H. Erikson in his book *Childhood and Society*. According to his theory, each separate life phase is marked by specific conflicts to be resolved, or lessons to be learned.[3] If the lessons which are taught are appropriate, then the odds are greatly increased that the child can successfully master the tasks of the next phase. However, if those lessons or patterns which are taught are wrong or unhealthy, then the probability is dramatically reduced that the child will be able to cope successfully with the following stages. Unfortunately, it is difficult to tell if a particular child is in fact learning lessons properly unless the parent/ caretaker observes him carefully. Often the fact that these lessons were not taught properly in the beginning only becomes apparent much later in a person's life.

The first lesson we learn, beginning at birth and lasting for the first year of life, concerns security. If our most basic needs for love, warmth, comfort and safety are provided, then we discover that our world is safe. If we are talked to, held, cuddled, and nurtured we are instilled with a sense of trust. When a child is neglected, his innate needs go unfulfilled. If these normal human needs are ignored long enough the child clearly perceives that he is not safe. He is indoctrinated to mistrust. If his cries for love continually evoke curt, negative replies or fall on deaf ears, in time his cries will end, and he simply fails to thrive. Unfortunately, the memories of these first lessons are very difficult to access in adulthood because they are stored deeply within the lower levels of the brain. This is because the more complex neurons of our higher brain centers continue to develop throughout the first year of life.

Our next lesson in life focuses upon our sense of personal power, or autonomy. This lesson is passed along to us, by our family or other teachers, between the ages of one and three. Here children begin to discover that they can have direct control over themselves, and influence their environment. Just as we begin to master our legs and toes in order to walk, we also begin to master our will in order to act. Children rapidly figure out how to assert this exhilarating power with great zeal. To be certain, we need to be taught limits to the expression of our will. However, if, during this phase, our wills are repeatedly denigrated, or destroyed, we never learn to run away, or scream loudly, even in those circumstances when we need to be able to do so for our own safety. If our basic instincts for self-protection are subverted we begin to doubt our perceptions. Why listen to the little voice in our guts which says, "Uh, oh! Danger!" if it does us no good? Why scream "No!" if no one is listening? Our abusers not only have coerced us into not trusting the world, but they have also brainwashed us into not trusting ourselves. If this is our indoctrination, then a potentially fatal infection of shame and doubt takes hold.

Building upon the previous lessons of security and personal power, the third phase of our instruction addresses self-determination, which typically spans ages three to six. Here a child's right to establish his budding sense of independence is either sustained and protected by his care-givers, or it is subjugated and crushed. Curiosity drives us to explore our world, often to the shock of a parent whose child has, within a matter of seconds, wandered out the door, up the ladder, and on to the roof just so they can see what the view is like from that altitude. "What is that?" children ask as they demand to know the name of everything they see. During this time of empowerment, children use play as a forum to discover their likes and dislikes. Blue crayons feel better in the hand than blue chalk. Blank paper is more fun to draw on than coloring books; so are walls! Here, children practice their skills and uncover their talents. They manifest a normal and natural impulse to create and to experiment. Scissors, glue, construction paper, and a little imagination can turn an ordinary cardboard box into a magic castle, or super-secret airplane hanger. Another question they expect an answer to is "Why?", as they try to make sense of this exciting, mysterious, and often confusing, place we call Earth.

However, if the child is refused the means to discover his preferences he will learn to be too compliant. If he is denied the opportunities to experiment he will learn to be too accepting of what others say. If he is blocked from the openness to explore he will learn to be too timid. If he is forbidden the time to question he will learn to be too passive. If those who instruct him let him know without a doubt that any question is a direct challenge to their authority, these dysfunctional teachers also instill within him the certain knowledge that nothing he does is good enough, and it is his fault. Instead of a healthy, and vital, sense of self-directedness, the child instead is inflicted with chronic guilt for simply, and naturally, being himself. Regardless of whether this is done out of ignorance or malice, if these perverse lessons are the ones the child is taught, he is literally being set up for the tragic role of "The Perfect Victim."

In the era of our education from ages six to twelve, the rush of time continues and we are thrust, ready or not, into an ever-increasing number of situations through which we struggle with the tasks of refining our life skills. By now we have become familiar with the differences which make us unique, and we begin to live our lives along these lines. Boys play with boys. Girls play with girls. These labels are useful in many situations, and can help us to gain a clearer sense of who we are in relation to others. They can also be used to separate and isolate us from others. Solitary play gives way to collective games and to rules. The delineation between winners and losers is made clear to us. This competition is also carried over into the classroom. The number and range of contacts outside the home continues to multiply exponentially through neighbors, friends, teachers, books, magazines, radio, and television. In this rapidly expanding environment we are suddenly faced with entirely foreign values, faiths, cultures, and languages.

Our responsibilities within the household become apparent as we are assigned duties. We also begin to discover the initially bizarre, but useful, concept of money and the power it brings. We might have an allowance, or our own small jobs in the neighborhood. In accomplishing the goals we choose for ourselves, we expand our power, exercise our rights, and discover our obligations. If the lessons of this era are well taught and sufficiently learned, we develop a sense of competency, or adequacy about ourselves.

But what if during this critical period we are robbed of these vital lessons by sexual abuse? Our grades begin to drop, and we are labeled "spaced-out," "lazy," "stupid," or "troubled." We have difficulty joining in familiar activities with the same enthusiasm. We probably will begin to withdraw into fantasy or depression. Not yet having the cognitive skills to relate intellectually, our emotions come out sideways in bed-wetting, nightmares, eating disorders, or acting-out behaviors. Confidence is replaced by inferiority. Competency becomes inadequacy. Belonging is traded in for isolation.

Even in the best of times, the final lesson of youth is difficult to master.

Starting at age twelve and lasting up to age eighteen, all the previous lessons are brought together to assist the young male to develop a solid self image. If previous instruction has been successful, the budding adult will begin to break his family ties and establish, for himself, a separate sense of individuality. While not totally independent, the need for a group identity takes on new importance during this time of transition. Bonding with others like himself, he discovers the meaning of teamwork, cooperation, decision making, and leadership.

The issue of sexuality takes on new dimensions as his body changes radically from that of a child to that of a young man. Hormones surge, bones stretch, muscles harden, beards sprout, and voices change. The strength to be vulnerable in an intimate relationship with another human becomes a necessary skill as he begins to play the dating game. In school he contemplates and defines the path his life will take next, whether it be a full-time job, additional vocational training, college, or the military. A healthy concern for others also emerges as he begins to understand that he, too, is an influential instructor as well as a responsible caregiver to those around him.

Conversely, if the abused male is abandoned to resolve questions concerning his self image and identity alone, he will be trapped in an overwhelming swamp of confusion. Yes, he depends upon others to meet his needs for warmth and love, but he doubts their sincerity. Yes, he relies upon others to help him gain his skills, but he does not fully trust anyone. Yes, he is part of the family and the community, but intuitively he senses that he does not belong. Yes, he has unique gifts and talents, but they are not good enough: they did not keep him safe, nor did they prevent someone from assaulting him. Yes, he has dreams and aspirations for the future, but he feels an overwhelming powerlessness to make them real. Yes, he has an undeniable right to choose for himself, but is helpless in the face of even mild opposition, and is even more helpless in situations where he needs to be strongly assertive. Yes, he has a body with feelings and sensations, but having disconnected himself from the pain in order to survive, he now has no voice, no arms and hands, no legs and feet. Yes, he is most assuredly male, but what does that mean? Is he destined to become like those who abused him? The effects of sexual abuse simply do not evaporate leaving behind no trace of contamination. Without skilled assistance to help him overcome the toxic effects of abuse, the confusion only compounds with each failed attempt to find freedom.

How Childhood Sexual Abuse Has Influenced My Social Life Area

Social problems_____

_____

_____

_____

_____

_____

_____

If you cannot think of a way to work on this issue directly, is there another Life Area which may help you cope with this problem indirectly?

Yes ___ No ___ Uncertain ___

If yes, what other Life Area might you use? How could this Life Area help you cope with this other problem?

Life Area _____

How _____

_____

_____

The person on my Recovery Team who might help me with this problem is

_____

The Economic Life Area

While at first it might appear improbable that childhood abuse could seriously influence adult financial realities, a closer examination proves this to be precisely the case. Denial, in any form, is never cheap. In many subtle, and not so subtle ways, being an untreated victim of childhood sexual abuse has determined not only our occupations and income levels, but our lifestyles, spending patterns, economic goals, and possibly even the level of physical comfort we allow ourselves.

Due to the effects of powerlessness and hopelessness, we may have decided there was no point in finishing high school, and we quit without earning a diploma. In doing so, we may have settled for dead-end jobs, never thinking about the fact that we were entitled to something better than what we had. If we did finish high school and continued on with our education, we may not have been able to make a clear commitment to any degree program because of our confusion and anxiety. Even after finding a career field in which we felt competent or comfortable, we did not push for promotions, raises, or retraining which we have earned, and we are due. Out of our negative self image, we failed to recognize opportunities for advancement and growth which were right in front of us. They did not exist in the first place because we simply believed we did not deserve them. Due to our passivity and/or propensity for being highly compliant, our very occupations could be nothing more than a form of re-victimization which is now being played out in the economic arena.

If we do not have a strong sense of the future, why should we consider savings accounts, insurance policies, retirement plans, or workable financial strategies? Having adapted to living in chaos, how many times have we moved in order to keep things exciting, or safe? What toll has the constant uproar in our lives taken upon our limited resources? On the opposite end of the scale, the financial successes achieved in life by some survivors can be directly related to an unending need for security, safety, recognition, approval, and control. In this dead-end situation, we are not living our lives out of freedom. Neither are we doing what we truly want. Rather, we are being driven forward simply because we do not see any other option. If this is the case, there most likely will come a time when the false security of financial safeguards slowly, but certainly, transforms into an economic prison of hollow wealth, or achievement.

How much money do you now spend on health care? If you suffer from chronic medical problems, is it possible they could be stress related? What about drug or alcohol abuse? What percentage of your income goes to numbing the pain? Good Scotch does have its price, and so do all avoidant behaviors. Have you ever had to pay fines for driving while intoxicated? What portion of your monthly income goes to supporting your desire for sexual excitement or pornography? How much time have you spent in treatment for depression, or other psychiatric problems? How much have you spent in the past months and years running from your inner realities? Take a look at your bank statements and tax returns for the past three, five, or ten years. They might have something to tell you. When I consider how much I spent maintaining my own denial before I entered Recovery, not to mention wasted time and effort, I shudder.

Running from our problems is not cheap, and neither is Recovery, but at least Recovery offers a positive return on our investments. Healing requires not only a directional shift in our energies, but also a serious rethinking of our financial resources and time. When you find a competent therapist, he or she will be worth every penny you pay them. These professionals have spent years in training, and like the rest of us, they have their own utility bills to pay. Taking private retreats, or heading off to conferences and workshops, requires us not only to spend our precious vacation days, but also demands an investment of dollars for food and travel. Recovery books and materials cost money. They take time and effort to read. Later on, as part of our overall Recovery, we may find it necessary and healthy to change jobs, obtain retraining, or continue with additional education. These expenses will need to be considered a part of our long-term budgets as well. While Recovery is not cheap, it is definitely worth the investment, since by now it has become painfully clear that the economic costs of denial, avoidance, and running away have simply become far too high.

At this point, the destructive impact of childhood sexual abuse upon just one adult survivor's economic situation is clear. However, if you multiply this reality by the estimated 10-15 million male survivors, plus the more than 25 million female survivors, the economic ramifications in the United States alone simply become numbing. What percentage of patients at state-funded psychiatric units were sexually abused? Maybe insanity was the only safe place they could find. How many clients at publicly supported mental health centers were assaulted before age 18? What is the figure that is paid out to survivors by private insurance companies for long-term therapy or other related problems? To what degree does childhood sexual abuse contribute to the overall number of cases of drug and alcohol abuse at treatment facilities subsidized by tax-payer dollars? In federally operated prisons, what percentage of the inmates were sexually abused as boys? Of the hundreds of thousands of homeless in this country, how many had to leave home as children because sleeping on a park bench was safer than sleeping in the room next to their father, mother, brother, or grandparent? How many already deceased AIDS victims were themselves molested long before the presence of the virus became front page news? No one knows, and I do not have any of the answers to these questions. However, I do know that each of these problems alone cost this country billions upon billions of tax dollars. This money, and more, will be required to address all of these issues. It is clear that in one way or another we all will continue to pay for the costs of childhood sexual abuse far into the foreseeable future.

On the global scale the scope is incomprehensible. Of the more than five billion humans on this planet, no insignificant number of them will be adult survivors of sexual abuse. One recent commentary concerning Vietnam's long-standing economic and social difficulties in recovering from the war attributed a significant proportion of that ongoing problem to a very high percentage of the population still suffering from chronic, war-related PTSD. If this, then, is true for that nation, how many poets, writers, healers, dreamers, leaders, artists, and scientists have we lost to the daily war which is silently waged against our children within the walls of our own homes? I can only dare to imagine the answer, and mourn the loss of untold lives and gifts which were never fulfilled, but should have been. For these unknown and nameless victims there is no black wall memorial in our nation's capital to remind us all of their battles fought, and lost.

How Childhood Sexual Abuse Has Influenced
My Economic Life Area

Economic problems_____

_____

_____

_____

_____

_____

_____

If you cannot think of a way to work on this issue directly, is there another Life Area which may help you cope with this problem indirectly?

       Yes ___ No ___ Uncertain ___

If yes, what other Life Area might you use? How could this Life Area help you cope with this other problem?

Life Area _____

How _____

_____

_____

The person on my Recovery Team who might help me with this problem is

_____

Step 4

◆

Self-Examination

We make a searching and courageous inventory of how sexual abuse has influenced our life and relationships, both now and in the past.

4th Step Strategies

During this Step please do not attempt to force yourself to remember any of the sexual abuse you experienced in the past. Let the child within you tell you what he remembers as he is able to do so. Let him tell you what he needs to tell you when he is ready. Personally, I think recovery of memory happens when it is safe to remember and there is a need in your Recovery to do so. It is not necessary for you to recall the exact hour, day and year of your abuse in order for you to successfully complete this Step. Children who are victims usually cannot supply this type of factual data because it is not a normal function of their mental abilities. They are just not psychologically wired to encode this type of information.

Therefore, if we would not reasonably expect a child to recall this information, then we should not expect this of ourselves. This is especially true for those of us who experienced the abuse at a very young age. It is even more true for those of us who were abused repeatedly for a number of years, or who were abused by several perpetrators. By working this Step our adult selves may be able to determine approximately when the abuse happened, but do not expect the child within you to give you these facts. He may not be able to do so. Again, let your inner self recollect what he can. Taking the 4th Step involves listening to your inner child in a calm, quiet, open manner. This is not an interrogation. The goal of this Step is to help free yourself from the negative influences of the abuse, not to force you into recalling the abuse itself. Whether you have complete and total awareness of everything that ever happened you, or you only have your certain, but unclear, gut feelings, this exercise will still be helpful. Keep in mind the four attitudes of journal work: patience, commitment, honesty, and courage.

It is tempting to leave out of your Life Review particular pieces of information because we are either embarrassed by them, or ashamed of them. If you are afraid that someone else may read those things which you have written down, then be careful where you keep your 12 Step Journal and how you carry it from place to place. If you wish, you do not have to place your name on it, nor do you have to identify specific people by their actual names. You could use initials or pseudonyms. Be careful, however, that you do not use this fear of someone's reading your Life Review as a reason for being anything but courageously honest with yourself. As someone once said, "We are only as sick as our secrets."

Courage is not a lack of fear or anxiety. Instead, it is having a great deal of fear and high levels of anxiety, and doing what we know needs to be done despite the sweaty palms, rapid heart beat, and knotted stomach. Keep in mind that you have already survived the abuse. Many of our past experiences will not come back to us in the ways in which we normally think of memory. With our adult minds we tend to think of recall in such concrete terms as who, what, where, when and how. Memory from childhood, however, is much more experiential. When we do have recall from childhood it will be through the eyes, ears, body, heart, and mind of the child we once were. We may not even be able to put such things into words at first. If you were abused before you learned to talk there is initially no language at all which will describe the past. Thus, these pre-verbal memories are much more likely to be a physical type of memory: some people call this "body memory." The mind cannot put words to what happened, but the body still carries the sensations once felt.

Another point to keep in mind during this Step is that any recall of the past, including the details of your sexual abuse, may not be especially sharp or entirely clear. Do not expect your memories to come back to you as if they were a seamless, perfectly focused movie. Indeed, your memories are most likely to be scattered, confused, jumbled, and disorganized. Impressions of people, places, things may tend to run together. Years and ages often overlap and fuse. Feelings are foggy and muddled. Because of the self-protective defenses of repression, suppression, and dissociation, major segments of the past have been edited from our conscious minds.

This editing typically includes a significant block of time both preceding and following the actual abuse, or abuses. Even in the best of circumstances, our conscious adult minds are capable of handling only a limited number of specific facts. Usually, this number ranges between five and ten. Under stress this range drops to just one or two separate items. Because of these expected mental limitations, along with our self-protective editing, we simply cannot expect ourselves to perfectly remember everything from the past on demand.

Another suggested strategy for working the 4th Step is to set some limitations on how long you plan to work on your Life Review. Be gentle with yourself, so do not sit down one day and attempt to complete the 4th Step in one sitting. But, it is very important that you set a reasonable time limit, such as several weeks or a month or so. This reconstruction of our past is an ongoing process. You will need time, a lot of time, as you work and rework this particular phase of healing.

Another possibility would be to set a specific limit on the number of times you work these exercises. One suggestion would be to set a limit at five, ten or fifteen Life Review sessions. These limits are necessary to help keep us on track and our efforts realistic. It would be easy for some of us survivors to spend our entire lives writing our autobiographies, and never get around to the rest of our healing. Remember, you can always return to this Step at a later time, and expand your Life Review.

At the end of this chapter **Options For Working The Life Review** explores alternate methods for handling this Recovery phase. My first Life Review was simply no more than a single sheet of paper with the names and dates of the towns and Air Force bases where I had lived during my childhood. At that point in my early Recovery, getting just that one single page completed took several sessions of intense detective work and some serious brain wracking, not to mention a lot of writing and rewriting. Since then I have added to and expanded my Life Review several times as my ability to recall the past has improved and other memories have returned.

For those adult survivors who have difficulty with dissociative states while completing their Life Review, the strategy of using Reality Checks may help you check-in when you have checked-out. During dissociative states we survivors are very much present in body, but our minds have drifted off to someplace else—often without our actually noticing this having happened. We may be experiencing flashbacks in one form or another. We might feel swamped by our inner hurricane of emotions and feelings. We also could be suffering from cognitive shutdown, or as someone once said, "a serious case of brain-lock."

A Reality Check helps you to get your brain running again, and to help you focus on the present. To do a Reality Check, first remind yourself what day of the week it is, or the month and year. Focus on your immediate environment by noticing the time of day, the season, the current temperature, or how the weather looks. Bring yourself back to your body by paying attention to what is occurring in your body. Ask yourself, "How do I feel?" Give yourself permission to become aware of the physical sensations of fear, anxiety, rage, or confusion which you were most likely experiencing just before you dissociated.

Also, do not forget to remind yourself to take a deep breath! Believe it or not, dissociation is something you can begin to control after some practice.

The final comments concerning the 4th Step involve the positive uses of denial, or in a more technical language, **encapsulation**. At times while working this Step you may begin to feel overloaded by the intense emotional content of returning memories or flashbacks. If you discover that your day-to-day life and functioning are becoming seriously impaired while working the 4th Step, then you might wish to consider using your denial to your benefit. This is not the same thing as re-entering denial!

By using encapsulation you affirm the reality of your memories and emotions, but are using your life-saving expertise at denial to keep the past from contaminating and paralyzing your life in the here and now. You are not putting off working this Step forever. Instead, you are consciously delaying your efforts until you can do so with your full energy. No one can do two things at once. Using this strategy is not a sign of failure. Rather, in a wise and realistic fashion, you have recognized the fact that there is only so much one person can do at any one time. This strategy is another way to help us to do first things first.

For example, you have a full-time job which you not only enjoy, but actually are good at doing. However, while working on the 4th Step you begin to find yourself distracted or even checking out while at work or the office. You could quit work and devote your full energies to completing the 4th Step, but then you would have the additional problems of not having money to buy food to eat and keep the electric bill paid. Besides, quitting your job to throw yourself into the 4th Step will not make your healing go any faster. This work is a process and takes time. While you cannot will a broken leg to heal, you can at least go easy on it, and yourself, as it mends.

Instead of setting yourself up for economic disaster, you might try to visualize a small box or briefcase in which you place your Recovery Journal. When you arrive at work, picture in your mind's eye leaving the box with your 12 Step Journal outside the door before going inside. During the day if you find that you are drifting off from your job duties, you can remind yourself that this is neither the time nor the place to do your Life Review. You can repeat to yourself over and over again that your 12 Step Journal is not in front of you, but outside.

If a memory does arise while at work, do not attempt to get into the heart of it right there and then. Jot down a few important facts on a scrap of paper, and put the note in your pocket. Later on you can then let yourself more fully explore this memory, but only after you have clocked out from work and gotten yourself back home, or to your safe place.

Some have used this technique by keeping their 4th Step work at one of their Recovery Team members' office, or home. You could do this same thing either in a literal fashion, or simply with your imagination. Encapsulation can also mean that you only work on this Step at a specific place once a week, or for a specific period of time such as the suggested half an hour or so once a day. To do part of your work on this Step, it might helpful to get away from your normal surroundings, and to take either a private or directed retreat. Whatever you do, make sure you are in a supportive environment.

If you are out visiting friends, again remind yourself that your job for the moment is to be relaxing and giving yourself a break, not working on the 4th Step. Stick your Recovery Journal in a desk and shut the drawer. At any point in our Recovery, taking a long and well deserved vacation is an excellent and highly recommended idea. We all need to recharge our batteries. However, make sure that you are truly on vacation and not mentally dragging your Recovery Journals around with you inside your head. By intelligently using encapsulation as a survival technique you will be setting yourself up for a more successful Recovery.

Preparing for the Life Review

With the suggested coping strategies in mind, now is the time to gather together the materials necessary for working the Life Review. First, you will need several sheets of paper modeled after the sample sheet provided at the end of this section. At the top of the sample page, you will notice three blanks. These are for you to write down the year you are examining, your age at that time, and the place or places you lived during that year. One way to do this is to write out this information on the top of a blank piece of paper. Another option is to make a master sheet modeled after the example, and photocopy as many pages as you may think you will need. You can then fill in the blanks as you go along.

Next, you will need both your 12 Step Journal, and at least one pencil with an eraser: in the beginning working in pencil, rather than pen, may be helpful. As the various impressions and memories from your past become clearer and more focused, you may need to re-date those pages, and move them to a different location within the Life Review. A pencil with an eraser makes such changes easier.

With your materials collected together, and your timer once again set for twenty minutes, begin to fill out the top of these pages as best you can, beginning with the year of your birth. If you are able to remember where you lived during those specific years then include this information as well. However, if your birthdate and recent times are the only things you can remember, then this is good enough. Just fill out the tops of the pages you have for those years which are available to you.

If you recall living in several different towns during any one single year, you may choose to use a different sheet for each separate location. Also, if there were significant changes within your family such as marriage, divorce, or death, these changes, too, may be noted on separate sheets. You always have permission to rearrange the chronological order of the pages in your Life Review as you feel necessary. You can always come back later and add new pages for additional memories as they arise. Use whatever arrangement feels comfortable and works for you. Remember, there is no one right, or wrong, way of organizing your Life Review. However, a simple Life Review usually works better than a complicated one.

You will notice that the remaining bottom portion of the sample page is lined, but otherwise blank. This remaining section of the page is reserved for you to write down the specific memories which you recall from the particular year you are examining. This will be discussed in more detail in the next section on **Working the Life Review**, so try not to get ahead of yourself by attempting to fill in these spaces at this point.

Working the Life Review

Having completed your preparations, you are now ready to start work on the main body of your Life Review. First, set your alarm clock, or timer, for half an hour. When your time is up, please put your pencil down, and close your Life Review. There are no absolute deadlines for this exercise. If the abuse did not kill you then, **remembering** it now will not kill you either. There is no rush. You have already survived the worst.

However, if at any time you feel that this exercise is becoming too intense, please stop immediately. For your own sake, remember that you have the right to stop doing something which either is not good for you, or you do not want to do. During this time if you should suddenly feel depressed, or suicidal, call one of your Recovery Team members immediately!

Remember that your recall of the past will not be very clear at times. Denial has taken its toll upon all of your memories, so do not be surprised if, in the beginning, it is difficult for you to recall much of anything. This is just as true for the good memories as for the difficult ones. If you become totally blank, return to the exercises concerning your Recovery Team, Recovery Journal, or Steps 1 through 3. Maybe there on those pages you will find the clues which will give you the starting points you need.

The opposite of this situation may also be true. You may experience any number of memories at once. If this happens to you, simply jot down a few key words or a phrase for each individual memory. Out of this list pick one and go with it. This technique will allow you to come back later and retrieve those remaining thoughts which have come to mind. The others which you have chosen not to address will still be there. You can return to them later when, and if, you choose to do so.

Trust the greater and wiser part of yourself to know when the time is right to let the memories surface, whether they are painful or pleasant. Include along with the factual aspects of the past the emotions you felt at the time. As one particular memory of a person, feeling, or fact comes to mind, quietly and calmly focus on that single memory. Remind yourself that you are in a safe place. Continue now to allow the one image that has come to mind to become clearer, and more full. Allow yourself to enter into that time and place, there in the past, as the person you once were.

Now as that single memory is present, find the proper page in your Life Review, and begin to write down on the paper in front of you the details of that one single impression. Take a deep breath and continue to allow yourself to let the image form within your mind's eye as you continue your writing. If you feel anxious about making a mistake, or getting all the details correct, take a deep breath, and relax. No one, except maybe yourself, expects you to get everything exactly right. You are not on trial. If you later realize that you have made a mistake concerning a particular place, person or time this is OK. Such corrections and clarifications in memory are normal. You can expect this to happen while you are working the Life Review. Again, that is why a pencil with an eraser is suggested.

Now that you have finished describing this, the first of your impressions, check your timer and see how much time you have remaining. If you do not feel that you have enough time left to continue, or feel that you are not ready to begin again, then put down your pencil, close your Life Review, and wait until your next scheduled 4th Step session.

If you feel that you have enough time left, and choose to continue, allow another thought or image to surface. You may also select one of the memory fragments which you jotted down earlier on your reminder list. With this memory becoming clearer, once again find the place and time that feels right within the pages of your Life Review. If you need to change pages, then do so now. Having found the proper page, begin to write this recollection down just as you have done with the one before. Continue with your writing until your time is up, or when you choose to stop.

Be sure that you stay committed to the 20-30 minute time limit that you have set for yourself. Also, be faithful to the boundaries you have established for working these exercises. When you have reached your self-determined stopping point for working this Step you will then be ready to consider moving towards the 5th Step.

Options for Working the Life Review

If you choose later to return and continue working on your Life Review, there are several alternatives, or options, which may help you fill in the blank spots of your past. The following section outlines a few of these. Do not feel that you have to do any of them. They are *only suggestions* for you to consider at some future point. Again, it is important for you to be in your safe place if you choose to do any of these exercises. Also, try to set some reasonable limits upon how much time, and maybe even money, you will spend on these optional Life Review exercises.

Photographs

Often an image captured on film communicates more clearly the spirit of another place and time than words ever could. Photographs often evoke long forgotten memories and powerful, buried emotions. If you have access to photos from your childhood you might consider putting together an album of these pictures. Unconsciously, you may literally have hidden them away in a box. Now might be a good time to pull them out and give the child you once were the recognition, honor and respect he is rightfully due.

The latest addition to my own Life Review was a painfully constructed album of family photographs which I was able to put together with the courageous help of my parents. They could have very easily refused to assist me. I am fortunate to have them present in my Recovery, as many survivors do not have a supportive family. There were so many places and dates I simply could not remember by myself. This photo album was not only expensive in terms of money for supplies and time for travel, but also emotionally exhausting.

If you have lost all records of your past due to the chaos of your adult years, but feel the need for some visual record, all is not entirely hopeless. There still are some possibilities to explore. You might bring a camera along with you to the town or neighborhood where you grew up and take some photos now. Much in the world has changed over the years, but you might be surprised by the number of things which have not. Your old house could still be there along with schools, play yards, parks, stores, libraries, hospitals, streets, and other landmarks. If little remains, a photograph of that town as it is now might still be helpful.

Schools, Libraries or Newpapers

You might think about contacting the Board of Education in your town of origin if you are searching for old class pictures, high school annuals, or school records. As a society we tend to keep files on everything. If you are unable to locate the address for the Board of Education, try the library. Public libraries are incredibly helpful in answering questions about all sorts of things, no matter how strange. If the Reference Librarian is unable to locate a particular address or phone number concerning these records, there is probably someone who does know where these materials might be found. Newspapers often have huge archives filed permanently on microfilm. Check with them and see if they have available any marriage or birth announcements, articles, obituaries, or photographs which might be helpful to you in your search.

There probably will be a reproduction cost to you in most cases, but it could be money very well spent. Whatever records you locate, make sure you treat them with respect. Spend some extra money and have them framed if you want to hang them on the wall of your home. If you wish, put them in a special binder or album to share with your friends, partner, support group, or Recovery Team. These pieces of the past could be very important to them and you in helping to understand more clearly the child you once were and the adult you are now.

Posters and Art Therapy

In *The Courage to Heal Workbook*, Laura Davis gives specific guidelines for using posters, or collages, as a means of expressing in visual form those emotions and memories from the past which simply cannot be communicated in words. She suggests gathering magazines with lots of full-page ads, scissors and glue. She also encourages survivors to give themselves plenty of working space and lots of time without interruptions. Exploring your emotions, memories and impressions in this manner can be especially meaningful.

A client of mine recently shared with me one of the more powerful posters I have ever seen. Rather than simply cutting out photographs from magazines and gluing them up in a flat, two-dimensional fashion, this person had come up with the idea of using pictures hidden under pictures to convey the layers of denial within the family. Covering the poster board there were little paper windows and doors which opened one after the other on to ever-deepening layers of personal truth and reality. On the surface were glossy images of happy, smiling faces; yet, buried beneath them where impressions of the all-too-familiar violence and abuse.

Art Therapy is a technique that I have found truly helpful, and believe me, I am no artist. Sometimes a particular memory fragment would stay with me for days, but no matter how much I tried, nothing new would come to mind. When I was able to sit down with a large drawing pad and a box of coloring pencils, I would often gain new details. Drawing pictures of your dreams, no matter how strange, can be another powerful tool for healing.

Working with Your Family or Friends

If your friends or family are not aware of your childhood sexual abuse and your efforts in Recovery, confronting them with this information is not only very difficult, but also extremely risky. In fact, confronting them with this reality could be outright dangerous to your well-being. If your family is not aware of your childhood sexual abuse, please see the material in Step 5 concerning **Confrontation**. It is very important that you review this material with your Recovery Team members before taking any such actions.

However, if friends or family are aware of your childhood sexual abuse, and they are supportive of your Recovery, they could be resources for working the 4th Step. Maybe they can remember things which you cannot. Also, they might have access to certain family histories, relationships, and secrets which may help you answer your personal questions of "Why...?" which in the past have eluded you. In forming your questions, try to think in terms of specific people, places, dates, relationships and interactions you need information about. One suggestion to help you do this is to use the newspaper reporter's habit of asking questions about Who, What, Where, When, How and Why.

Life Review

Year_____ Age _____ Place(s)_____

Memories of people, places and things.

_____

_____

_____

_____

_____

_____

_____

_____

_____

_____

_____

_____

_____

_____

_____

_____

_____

_____

Step 5

---◆---

Admission

We admit to our Higher Power, to ourselves, and to another person the exact nature of how sexual abuse has influenced our life and relationships both now and in the past.

Many times when we hear the word "admit," we think of a courtroom and a criminal confessing his crimes. Here in the 5th Step, however, admission is intended to mean we acknowledge the reality of how sexual abuse has influenced our life and our relationships, both in the past and in the present. By declaring these truths we continue to challenge the denial which has controlled our lives. As we confirm the facts, we bear witness to the realities we have had to face and carry.

In order for us to take this Step, we begin to assert the right to reclaim the personal power which was stolen from us long ago. Throughout history, there have been many myths and legends which speak of this resurrection of spirit and reclamation of divine right. In Recovery, one of the tasks we face is the reawakening of our Inner Warrior.[1] This image can be disturbing for survivors since we have only seen the dark, destructive aspects of control, strength, will, and single-mindedness. We have never been shown how to use these qualities for growth and healing.

In taking the 5th Step, we learn that control does not always mean manipulation. Appropriate control can empower us to stand against the abuse of the past in the presence of our Higher Power and our 5th Step Sponsor. We can begin to say "NO!" to those who wished to harm us, and "YES!" to those who offer us support, love, joy and courage. As our Inner Warrior awakens from his long sleep, our single-mindedness of purpose does not have to be blind to the needs of others. Our resolute dedication of purpose can hold us steady when we falter and keep clear the vision of our goals.

This Step involves many possible levels. The first of these is sharing our personal reality with our Recovery Team. Another level might include sharing with our partner, friends, or family. The most complicated and maybe dangerous is confronting those who abused us. **Confrontation is not a requirement for taking this Step**. Some of us will decide to delay confrontation until later in our Recovery. Others will determine the risks outweigh any possible gains. Neither decision is absolutely right or wrong. Each is simply different, as each of our needs is different. The goal of this Step is to reclaim our personal power. The decision to confront is something which must be made only after we have explored all possible options, considered the risks, examined our expectations, and sought out the advice of others.

Taking this Step is a deliberate challenge to the powerful taboo of speaking about the unspeakable. A portion of ourselves still feels that something horrible and awful will happen if we break the silence; therefore we need to examine the issues of confidentiality, place, and time in order to resolve these fears.

PREPARING FOR THE 5TH STEP

What To Say and How To Say It

There is no single right or wrong way of sharing with another person our 4th Step material from the last chapter. We may not be able to read aloud the words we have written. This not a sign of failure, but rather the best we can do at this early stage of Recovery. A list of possible options for sharing this information with your chosen Team Member has been included for your evaluation at the end of this section. Read the list and rank these options from most comfortable and safe to least desirable.

Our 5th Step Sponsor

The person we choose as our sponsor is a matter for careful consideration as this can be an especially emotional time. The very idea of sharing our histories with another person can provoke intense feelings, and it is not uncommon for survivors to develop physical symptoms. I would suggest you delay taking this Step until there is a Recovery Team member you can trust with this information and who can competently support you.

Confidentiality is very important and needs to be discussed openly and honestly. If the person you ask to be your 5th Step sponsor cannot assure you that what you share will be held in the strictest confidence, you may need to consider another person. If this person is willing to assure confidentiality, then you can negotiate with him/her some limits on time, and explore options for place.

When We Will Work The 5th Step

As in the 4th Step, it is important to set some specific time limits. This can be done by allowing yourself a certain number of 5th Step sessions or by limiting the number of days or weeks you will work on this Step.

Setting these limits is helpful for several reasons. First, it gives your sponsor a clear idea about what is expected and he/she will be more able to honestly say yes or no to your requests. Secondly, it is important that we affirm positive control. Giving ourselves a predetermined starting and stopping point helps us to maintain our focus.

Where To Take The 5th Step

Where we choose to work our 5th Step is also a helpful consideration. For each of us, some places are more familiar and secure than others. Give yourself permission to create an image that feels warm, safe, secure, and comfortable. Think about how you might be able to re-create those qualities which seem important. As you examine the list of possible places, consider those which most appeal to you.

Symbols Of Strength And Protection

Symbols can be very useful tools in helping us feel more secure and powerful. A brief list of symbols has been provided at the end of this section to help you think about the available possibilities. Such symbols are highly personal and carry a great deal of emotional meaning, even if they do not make much rational sense. If you find yourself attracted to one of those mentioned put a check by it. Then you can begin to think about how you might incorporate these personal symbols into your strategies for taking the 5th Step.

After Taking the 5th Step

As you consider the issue of time, give some serious thought to scheduling a post-session block of time of several hours or a day or so. This post-session time would allow you to consider any changes you would like to make the next time you take the 5th Step. This includes the issues of sponsorship, time, place, and symbols. As your Recovery continues, the means by which you take the 5th Step will evolve. By being aware of those things you would, or would not, change in taking this Step, you develop an awareness of how you are growing and changing.

Such a time also gives you an opportunity to listen to your reactions, thoughts, and feelings. It is common to have very powerful emotional reactions, so it may be wise to consider maintaining contact with your 5th Step sponsor or other members of your Recovery Team.

5th Step Exercises

1. The following list explores the various options available for taking the 5th Step with member/s of your Recovery Team. Rank them from the most comfortable/safe (#1) to least comfortable/safe (#10).

_____ Write my sponsor a letter and let him or her read it out loud to me.

_____ Write my sponsor a letter and I read it out loud to him or her.

_____ Let my sponsor read selections from the 12 Step exercises I have completed in my Recovery Journal.

_____ Read out loud to my sponsor selections from the 12 Step exercises I have completed in my Recovery Journal.

_____ Share with my sponsor those paragraphs or sections from this book which I feel especially apply to me.

_____ Share with my sponsor those paragraphs or sections of other books or articles which I feel especially apply to me.

_____ Share with my sponsor my 4th Step photo album.

_____ Share with my sponsor my 4th Step poster.

Other Ideas Not Listed

_____ A. _____

_____ B. _____

2. Who on your Recovery Team might be willing to sponsor you when you take the 5th Step?

A. _____

B. _____

C. _____

After you have considered your list of names, and have talked with each about his or her willingness to help you with this Step, who is the person/s you have chosen as your sponsor in taking the 5th Step for the first time?

Name: _____

Other Recovery Team Members to be present as witnesses (this is an option which may or may not be appropriate depending upon your circumstances):

Name: _____

Name: _____

3. After my 5th Step sessions, how much time will I give myself to think about and integrate what was said and done?

I will give myself _____ hours.

After my 5th Step sessions, the person I will talk to who will help me process this aspect of my Recovery is:

Name: _____

4. Where will I be doing my 5th Step work with this member of my Recovery Team?

___ his/her office	___ his/her home
___ my office	___ my home
___ church	___ retreat facility
___ a park	___ the woods
___ the ocean	___ the mountains
___ the desert	___ an open field
___ Other options	

A. _____

B. _____

5. What symbols of strength and protection can I use to help me feel secure and powerful in taking the 5th Step?

___ candle	___ incense
___ bonfire	___ holy water
___ favorite blanket	___ favorite pillow
___ robe	___ written ceremony
___ religious icons	___ protective talisman
___ prayer beads	___ walking staff
___ 12 Step Recovery Journal	___ Daily Recovery Journal
___ books	___ close friend/partner

___ favorite photograph of myself as a child

___ other members of my Recovery Team

___ Other items to help me feel safe and comfortable

A. _____

B. _____

6. Now that I have completed my 5th Step, what things would I change the next time I work this Step? (for example: sponsorship, the number of sessions, the length of the sessions, the days or weeks allotted, place where the 5th Step was taken)

A. _____

B. _____

C. _____

D. _____

Confrontation

We survivors have lived so long in unsafe situations that, we may not realize we are moving into deep and dangerous waters once more. Because of our denial, we may not be aware of those self-protective intuitions which usually warn us if someone does not have our best interests in mind. Out of our grief and loss, we may still hold on to the unrealistic expectation that our families really are "OK" if we can just give them one more chance. If we have not yet reached the point in our Recovery where we have examined our expectations, challenged our unrealistic fantasies, developed our intuition, and learned how to protect ourselves, we may be simply fulfilling our pattern of revictimization.

As I noted earlier in the book, bad help is worse than no help at all, so I want to offer the best advice I can on this subject. Of all materials I have seen (and used myself) concerning the issues of revelation and confrontation, there are two resources which I feel are required reading for survivors and their Recovery Team members. The first of these is *The Courage to Heal Workbook* by Laura Davis. The chapters "Confrontations" and "Dealing With Your Family Now" offer specific exercises which are well developed, and proven. I would not recommend that you reveal your childhood sexual abuse to your partner and/or friends until after you have read the sections in this book which address these issues. The second resource, by no means less valuable than the first, is *Victims No Longer* by Mike Lew. Within the chapter "Confrontation," he clearly discusses the pros and cons, offers advice for those situations when the perpetrator is dead, and honestly examines what can go wrong in a confrontation.

If you are considering confronting your family and/or abuser(s), and have not reviewed at least one of these resources with your Recovery Team, you may be setting yourself up for great emotional pain, or even physical harm. Many survivors have had extremely traumatic experiences in confronting their families and/or their abuser(s). Our failing to learn from their painful lessons is both dangerous and unnecessary.

Step 6

---◆---

Healing

We willingly ask our Higher Power to heal our pains due to abuse and to free us from the effects these pains continue to have upon our adult lives.

On the surface this Step is deceptively easy. It takes less than a minute to read the words, but requires a lifetime to make manifest. In the very beginning I desperately wanted to go through this Step just once, get it over with, and go on. I am a bit wiser now, and can accept the truth that I will spend the rest of my life in Recovery. We consciously choose to continue on with our healing by practicing Affirmations and setting Goals. Recovery is a matter of learning how to exercise our freedom of choice.

This chapter goes to the heart of such basic issues as control, fear and trust. For us survivors control is a big issue. People, places, and things often scare us. In order to feel safe we have developed extraordinary skills in directing the course of our lives. We tend to either make ourselves invisible or allow others to get only so close before we put up our defensive shields. We also have learned how to keep a tight rein on emotions, monitor our thoughts, or pretend we are not feeling anything bad at all. Even thinking about letting go of control is unsettling.

Trusting anyone, including ourselves, is extremely difficult. Trusting our Higher Power is at times nearly impossible. There may be a part of us which suspects the abuse we suffered was the will of our Higher Power. If this is the case, how could we willingly ask Him to heal us? How can we submit to Him for renewal? Taking this Step often involves an intense struggle between that aspect of ourselves which holds on to the hope of a miracle, and that portion frozen by helplessness. Yet, in the struggle, we can begin to learn to trust. The resources for our renewal already exist deep within us, though dormant for so many years we may doubt their existence.

Working the 6th Step often feels like being on an island threatened by a large storm. The seas are too dangerous and choppy for rescue by boat. The only escape option is flying out by plane. I can either stay and risk riding out the storm, or I can board the next flight. If I choose to take the plane, I am entrusting myself to the pilot, air-traffic controllers and ground crew. After buckling the seat belt, the only thing I can do is take a deep breath and trust that everybody knows exactly what he or she is doing.

More times than I can count during my own Recovery, I have found myself experiencing what I call the "Ah, Ha! — Oh, Shit . . . Syndrome." It usually goes something like this. I struggle and struggle with a problem, and eventually perceive what part of my life causes this difficulty. "Ah, Ha! Now I see what is going on here! I am stuck on an island and another storm is coming!" After this revelation, however, the second half of the syndrome kicks in, and I say to myself, "Oh, Shit! Now what do I do? How can I get off this island as soon as possible?" At this point I have a choice. My first option is to panic and try to figure out the entire problem all by myself. This usually does not work too well since if I knew what to fix, and how to do it, I would not be in this mess to begin with. My second choice is to take a deep breath, trust my Higher Power, and work the 6th Step once more by practicing my Recovery Affirmations and setting Recovery Goals.

Recovery Affirmations

Making affirmations is a very powerful tool for healing. These declarations help us to develop a new vision of possibilities for our own lives. Often we are convinced that the past which we have endured is the future we must face. This is not true, but to acquire new perspectives we must challenge the old ones unconsciously held for so many years. At the beginning of our Recovery, we are usually not aware of those beliefs which have directed our lives. We may never have been told these things in words, but we got the message, and learned the lessons far too well: "There is no safe place to go," "I do not deserve love," "I am unworthy of healing," "No one can help me," "Nothing can change."

One example of a Recovery Affirmation is, "I deserve the gift of healing from my Higher Power." Such an affirmation helps us to see that we truly do have the right to heal. It helps us to challenge false perceptions which have limited our lives, and imprisoned our spirits. The act of affirming our right to heal is an expression of renewal. By making this pronouncement we begin to claim this gift from our Higher Power. By selecting and practicing our Recovery Affirmations we are literally changing the way we see the world and our place in it. Included with this chapter is a list of Recovery Affirmations designed to reinforce the forgotten truths about ourselves. At first they may seem foreign, artificial, or phony, but they will become more real through repetition. If none of these seems appropriate, feel free to adapt them to your own unique circumstances.

There are many valid ways of practicing Affirmations. One is to write your chosen Recovery Affirmations on several small cards. Place these cards where you will see them regularly as reminders. Some individuals use their Affirmations as a type of silent mantra or meditation. Others find it helpful to say their Affirmations out loud to themselves in a mirror or in the presence of a Recovery Team member.

Recovery Goals

An example of a Recovery Goal is, "I will set aside twenty minutes a day for Daily Inventory (10th Step)." Such goals help us to make concrete the Affirmations we practice. Our actions, behaviors, habits, and speech will reflect the truth of our Affirmations as they become more a part of our being. The realization of these Goals is often slow and frustrating. We work and work, but nothing seems to be changing. Yet, any positive effort, no matter how small, sets the stage for the next transformation. If we continue to stay with our goals something eventually does happen, and the almost invisible changes begin to add up and multiply. A chain reaction of healing begins to take place. Ultimately, a critical mass is reached and we break through those barriers which have held us back for so long.

To help make our Recovery Goals tangible, we can thoughtfully examine the past and begin to contemplate concrete changes we would like to make in our lives. Some questions you might consider are: How do I want my life to be different within the next few months, or years? Where will I be if I do not make any changes? Which Life Area seems to need the most immediate attention? To help define these objectives more clearly you might wish to examine your work in the previous Steps. Be as specific as possible. Try to phrase your Recovery Goals in terms of who, what, where, when, and how. You might ask your Recovery Team members to help you meet these specific Recovery Goals. As these plans for the future evolve, write them down and believe they can become real as your Recovery continues.

Psychological Affirmations for Recovery

My wounded inner child has the right to be healed.
He has the right to be safe, whole, spontaneous, and
life-filled once again.

———◆———

My wounded inner child has the right to be at peace
within myself.
My wounded inner child has the right to be treated with
gentleness, kindness, patience and compassion.

———◆———

My inner child has the right to scream, yell, cry, and be
angry about the things that happened in the past.
I am an adult. I am a Man. I have the power and
strength to protect the scared little boy within me.

———◆———

I have the right to trust myself.

———◆———

I have the right to listen to my intuition.

———◆———

I have the right to think logically.

———◆———

I have the right to challenge hopelessness.

———◆———

I have the right to challenge helplessness.

———◆———

I have the right to challenge powerlessness.

———◆———

I have the right to challenge confusion.

———◆———

I have the right to resolve my conflicts.

I have the right to be relaxed and calm.

———◆———

I have the right to feel anger/rage.

———◆———

I have the right to discharge this anger/rage in safe,
non-destructive ways.
I have the right to feel scared and worried.

———◆———

I have the right to mourn and feel sadness.

———◆———

I have the right to laugh and giggle.

———◆———

I have the right to play.

———◆———

I have the right to be creative.

———◆———

I have the right to be different.

———◆———

I have the right to a peaceful night's sleep.

Psychological Goals for Recovery

*By the end of the month I will either make for myself,
or purchase for myself, a large housecoat in my
favorite color.*

*By the end of the month I will give to myself the gift of a
stuffed Teddy Bear.*

*By the end of next month I will give to myself a really
nice blanket to curl up in when I am feeling scared.*

*Within the next six months I will think about the kind of
pet which best suits my present lifestyle.*

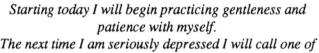

*Starting today I will begin practicing gentleness and
patience with myself.
The next time I am seriously depressed I will call one of
my Recovery Team members or an emergency crisis line.*

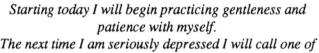

*The next time I have the compulsion to go get drunk,
stoned, loaded, or high I will contact one of my
Recovery Team members before I do so.
By the end of three months I will have asked at least two
of my friends to see if they know of any good therapists
they can recommend.*

*By the end of three months I will have interviewed at
least one therapist to see if I want him or her on my
Recovery Team.*

*By the end of the year I will have made plans for a
five-day vacation to one of my favorite places.*

*By the end of the year I will have made plans for a
weekend trip to a place where I have never been before.*

*Within the next year I will try to take off one extended
weekend every three months just to be alone and quiet.*

*Beginning next month I will give myself permission to
have one day a week to take care of my home.*

*Within the next four months I will do something creative
just for me (painting, pottery, drawing, photography,
furniture making, stained-glass making, sculpture,
writing, music, dance, cooking, or gardening).*

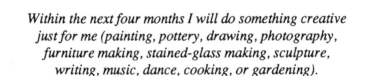

*The next time I am scared at night
I will plug in a night light.*

Spiritual Affirmations for Recovery

I deserve the gift of spiritual healing.

◆

I deserve the gift of joy.

◆

I deserve the gift of serenity.

◆

I deserve the gift of renewal.

◆

I deserve the gift of transformation.

◆

I deserve the gift of wisdom.

◆

I deserve the gift of wholeness.
I deserve the gift of growth.

◆

I deserve the gift of resurrection.

◆

I deserve the gift of enlightenment.

◆

I deserve the unconditional love of my Higher Power.

◆

I deserve the unconditional forgiveness of my Higher Power.

◆

I deserve the unconditional presence of my Higher Power.

I have the right to a relationship with my Higher Power as I understand Him.

I have the right to be in solitude to spend time alone with my Higher Power.

I have the right to experience my spiritual self.

I have the right to claim my spiritual gifts.

I have the right to claim my spiritual talents.

I have the right to choose my spiritual tradition.

I have the right to choose my spiritual advisors.

I have the right to choose my spiritual family.

I have the right to choose my spiritual practices.

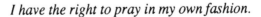

I have the right to pray in my own fashion.

I deserve to be listened to when I am talking about my spiritual concerns.

Spiritual Goals for Recovery

I will try to find within the next year a spiritual advisor I feel I can trust to be on my Recovery Team.

Starting today, I will begin to think about how I can establish a realistic time and place for some daily silence and solitude.

The next time I dissociate during a religious ceremony I will try to use the Reality Check techniques to bring myself back into my body.

Once a month I will go to a safe church building and sit quietly for twenty minutes.

By the end of four months I will have talked to my spiritual advisor about my wanting to take a private retreat sometime within the next year.

Beginning today I will begin to practice being gentle and patient with myself concerning my spiritual growth.

I will make plans within the next month to have my own private service alone down by the lake at sunrise.

By the end of the week I will have called three gift shops to see if I can find a copy of the Serenity Prayer to hang on my bedroom wall.

Before I move into my new home I will talk with my spiritual advisor about having a house-blessing ceremony.

Within the next three months I will have asked at least one of my friends if they would be willing to pray to their Higher Power for healing and renewal on my behalf.

Sexual Affirmations for Recovery

I deserve the gift of sexual healing.

I do not deserve sexual relationships which are abusive.

*I have the right to end any relationship I feel is
sexually abusive.*

I deserve to feel comfortable about my adult sexuality.

I deserve to become aware of my own sexuality.

I deserve to become aware of my own body.
*I have an obligation to myself, and others, to be respon-
sible for my sexuality and my sexual behavior.*

I have the right to be celibate.

*I have the right to be sexually assertive, and to say
"No" when I am uncomfortable with any sexual
requests.*

I deserve to be treated with tenderness, and patience.

I have the right to reclaim my masculine self.

I have the right to reclaim my feminine self.

*I deserve positive emotional support without the
expectation that I will have sex.*

I have the right to decide for myself what sexual practices I will, and will not, be involved in. I have the right to change my mind about these matters whenever I wish.

I have the right to tell someone to stop doing something if I am uncomfortable.

I have the right to tell someone to stop doing something if I am scared or nervous.

I have the right to decide if I will be kissed.

I have the right to decide how I will be kissed.

I have the right to decide if I will be touched.

I have the right to decide how I will be touched.

I have the right to decide if my penis is touched.

I have the right to decide how my penis is touched.

I have the right to decide if my anus is touched.

I have the right to decide how my anus is touched.

I have the right to expect that my self-determination will be respected.

I have the right to be educated and informed on sexual matters.

Sexual Goals for Recovery

Until I learn what sexual practices are considered high risk and which ones are considered safer, I will choose to remain sexually celibate.

By the end of the week I will have found out what sexual practices are considered safe and high-risk.

Beginning today I will begin to take responsibility for my sexual behavior.

Within the next three months I will talk to a member of my Recovery Team about my wanting to reconnect with my sexual self.

Within the next four months I will talk to a member of my Recovery Team about helping me to discover other ways of meeting my emotional needs other than through sexual behavior.

Within the next two months I will make a list of the things in the sexual relationship with my lover or partner about which I feel uncomfortable/comfortable.

Within the next four months I will try to share that list with my lover or partner.

The next time I masturbate I will focus on my body and try not to check out or escape into fantasy.

*During the next six months when I am having sex with
my lover or partner I will tell him or her to stop what he
or she is doing if I become aware of my feeling
uncomfortable or anxious.*

◆

*Within the next year I will read at least two
non-pornographic books on sexuality.*

◆

*The next time I feel that I am about to give in to any
sexual compulsion that involves unsafe sex I will contact
one of my Recovery Team members before I do so.*

◆

*The next time my partner or lover asks me to have sex
I will not automatically tell her or him "Yes." Instead I
will give myself permission to think about the request
and to ask myself if this something I am interested
in right now.*

Physical Affirmations for Recovery

I deserve the gift of physical healing.

———◆———

I deserve a long and fulfilling life.

———◆———

I deserve a life free from chemical addictions.

———◆———

I deserve a life free from alcohol abuse.

———◆———

I deserve a life free from illegal drug abuse.

———◆———

I deserve to be free from eating disorders.

———◆———

I have the right to listen to my physical hunger.

———◆———

My body deserves healthy foods.

———◆———

My body deserves a balanced diet.

———◆———

I deserve to feel comfortable about my body.

———◆———

I deserve to enjoy the gifts of my physical senses.

———◆———

I have the right to experience pleasure.

———◆———

I have the right to be surrounded by things which nurture and comfort me.

I have the right to hear the kind of music I find healing.

◆

I have the right to enjoy silence.

◆

I have the right to determine if I will be touched.

◆

I have the right to determine when I will be touched.

◆

I have the right to determine who will touch me.

◆

I have the right to determine how they will touch me.

◆

I have the right to say "No!" when someone asks to touch me.

◆

I have the right to say "Yes!" when someone asks to touch me.

◆

I have the right to ask someone to hold my hand.

◆

I have the right to ask someone to hug me.

Physical Goals for Recovery

Within the next month I will talk to one of my Recovery Team members about my difficulties with drugs or alcohol.

I will remain drug-free just one day at a time.

I will remain alcohol-free just one day at a time.

Starting today I will try to become aware of how much coffee I drink.

Starting today I will try to become aware of how many cigarettes I smoke.

By the end of four months I will have talked to at least one member of my Recovery Team about what options are available for massage therapy, or other types of body work.

Once a day I will try to spend ten minutes focusing upon how my body feels.

Beginning today I will give myself permission to enjoy things which look, feel, sound, smell and taste good.

By the end of the month I will have figured out where I can hang a punching bag to beat on when I am hurt or angry.

The next time I am upset or anxious I will take a long hot shower to help me relax instead of watching television.

———◆———

The next time I know I will be in a stressful situation I will practice staying in my body by focusing upon my breathing rather than "checking out" automatically.

———◆———

Within the next two weeks I will try to find the time to go for a twenty-minute walk three times a week.

———◆———

Once a week I will give myself permission to go to bed early and to sleep late.

———◆———

Over the next six months I will try to eat only when I am hungry, and to eat only enough to satisfy the hunger.

———◆———

During the next three months I will make plans to change doctors because the one I am seeing now does not take me seriously.

———◆———

The next time I see my attending physician I will tell him how much I appreciate his taking the time to listen to my problems and answer my questions.

Social Affirmations for Recovery

I deserve the gift of social healing.

I deserve to be at peace with myself and others.

———◆———

I deserve supportive relationships.

———◆———

I do not deserve to be in an abusive relationship.

———◆———

I have the right to end a relationship that is abusive in any manner or fashion.

———◆———

I have the right to protect myself.

———◆———

I have the right to learn how to protect myself in positive ways.

———◆———

I have the right to choose when I will, and will not, visit with my family of origin.

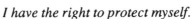

I have the right never to see my family of origin again.

———◆———

I have the right as an adult to create for myself a new and loving family.

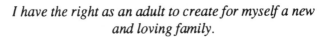

I have the right to choose my friends.

I deserve to be surrounded by loving people.

I have the right to choose where I live.

———◆———

I have the right to live in a warm, dry, and safe home.

———◆———

I have the right to set limits with my time.

———◆———

I have the right to choose when I will do things.

———◆———

I have the right to set limits with my space.

———◆———

I have the right to privacy.

———◆———

I have the right to be alone.

———◆———

I have the right to unplug my phone.

———◆———

I have the right to get an unlisted phone number.

———◆———

I have the right to choose where I will do things.

———◆———

*I have the right to determine with whom I will spend
my time.*

Social Goals for Recovery

Within the next year I will talk to one of my Recovery Team members about attending a Recovery support group.

Within the next four months I will make plans to end my relationship with (name of person) because he/she does not support my Recovery efforts.

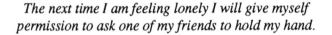

The next time I am feeling lonely I will give myself permission to ask one of my friends to hold my hand.

———◆———

The next time someone says he/she wants to touch me I will tell him/her not to touch me if I really do not want him/her to touch me.

———◆———

The next time one of my family members expects me to call or visit, I will ask myself if this is something I really want to do.

———◆———

The next time one of my family members wants to visit me I will not automatically agree to this request. I will tell him or her I will call back in a few hours after I have had time to check my schedule for those days. Before I confront my family with the truth about the childhood sexual abuse I suffered I will talk to at least one of my Recovery Team members about how to handle this situation. We will set aside four sessions to explore this issue.

Within the next six months I will make plans to move from the place I am living.

For the next two years I will make plans to stay where I am presently living and not move.

Within the next year I will ask at least one of my friends to go with me to a karate, aerobics, or yoga class.

During the next six months I will try to accept the good things my friends give me without feeling that I have to return the favors immediately.

Beginning today I will begin to challenge the false belief that I can make people happy or sad. I am not their Higher Power.

Beginning today I will begin to challenge the false belief that people can make me happy or sad. They are not my Higher Power.

Economic Affirmations for Recovery

I deserve the gift of economic healing.

◆

I deserve economic stability.

◆

I have the right to use my economic resources to help me reach my other Recovery Goals.

◆

I have the right to develop long-term economic goals.

◆

I have the right to ask for well-informed economic advice.

◆

I have the right to create my own budget.

◆

I have the right to change my budget.

◆

I have the right to start a savings account.

◆

I have the right to develop a retirement plan.

◆

My co-workers are not my family of origin.

◆

Where I work is not the house/place where I was abused.

◆

I have the right to be treated with respect and dignity on my job.

I deserve to feel good about what I do for a living.

———◆———

I have the right to change jobs.

———◆———

I have the right to change careers.

———◆———

I have the right to further my education.

———◆———

I have the right to further my occupational training.

Economic Goals for Recovery

At the end of twelve months I will have made a decision either to stay at my current job, or to find a new one.

At the end of two years I will have made a decision either to go back to school for more education, or to take training for a new career field.

Within the next six months I will talk to at least one member of my Recovery Team about what kind of job would best suit my gifts and talents.

Over the next twelve months I will make plans to change jobs because my employer is abusive and has not changed his behaviors even after I confronted him with this.

The next time I feel that I am being mistreated on my job I will discuss this matter with a member of my Recovery Team to help me see how best to handle this resentment.

Over the next nine months I will review my actual expenses in order to determine where I am really spending my money.

Within six weeks I will have evaluated three different computer software packages in order to determine which one is best suited to helping me keep up with my budget.

Within the next four months I will have talked to at least one member of my Recovery Team about establishing a budget.

Within the next year I will read at least one book about personal finances.

Beginning today I will think about how much money I spend on things which I really do not need.

By the end of next month I will decide how much money I can realistically set aside out of my budget to finance my Recovery (books, workshops, therapy, travel, etc.).

Within the next six months I will talk to two different financial advisors about the options available for starting a retirement account.

———◆———

Within the next six months I will decide what percentage of my income I can set aside into a savings account to cover such things as an emergency, a job change, or a vacation.

Step 7

◆

Forgiveness

We humbly ask our Higher Power to forgive us of our shortcomings with ourselves and others caused by childhood abuse and adult patterns of denial.

If there has been one single Step which has caused me the most turmoil, confusion, frustration and sheer spiritual anguish, it has been the 7th Step. After my remembering the abuse I was desperately searching for some way of coping with it, and in the beginning I almost rejected the 12 Steps altogether because of this Step. A part of myself wanted to forgive in order to forget. Another part knew I could never, and should not ever, forgive and forget. Out of this struggle I believe there is a perspective which allows me to validate the reality of the pain and at the same time move onward with Recovery. This involves examining the issue of Forgiveness through the eyes of The Martyred Child, The Guardian Parent, and The Compassionate Heart of our Higher Power.

The Martyred Child

The image of the Martyred Child was brought home to me quite powerfully while on retreat at the Abbey of Gethsemani. Toward the end of my stay came the Feast Day of Saint Agatha, an early martyr of the Christian Church. In the homily for the morning Mass the attending priest told how Agatha, at the time of her conversion, vowed her chastity to God as a symbol of her faith. Later in life, she was given the choice either to surrender her symbol of faith and live, or to retain her virginity and die. She chose to keep her faith and face death. The priest continued by drawing the parallels between St. Agatha's willing martyrdom for her beliefs, and the silent unseen martyrs who are the abused children in our current world. As he said these words an audible gasp rose from some of those present. His closing prayer was for today's unwilling martyrs of childhood abuse to find the same peace, healing and release St. Agatha had found in the Resurrection.

During the Communion which followed, I looked up to discover mine were not the only eyes filled with tears. As the Mass ended I watched others leave the chapel sobbing in silence. A disturbing awareness struck me that I was not the only adult survivor present in the morning's service. Statistically, it was probable that some of the monks, as well as a number of the other retreatants, had also been abused as children. Shaken, I returned to my room and grieved.

Some things we must remember. To forget is to sentence the next generation to suffering the same pain, and to doom them to repeating the same tragic mistakes. To forget is also to forsake the lives of those who have been martyred. There are episodes in our collective human experience which are so obscene, mindless and bestial that it is easy to deny that they are real or even that they happened. History is filled with such examples: Auschwitz, Dachau, Dresden, Hiroshima, Nagasaki, The Trail of Tears, and The Killing Fields to name a few. Each of these is just as inhuman today as it was then, and it will be just as inhuman tomorrow. In the same manner childhood abuse was, is, and always will be horribly wrong. In this sense we must never forget.

However, there are some things to be considered if our identity is based solely upon that of the Martyred Child. Over the years I have seen some victims of abuse who remained victims their entire lives. They so identified with their Martyred Child that they were either unable or unwilling to allow themselves to enter into Recovery and experience healing. Tragically, I have also seen a few cases where individuals actually used their childhood victimization as an excuse to justify their out-of-control behavior. In such situations the result is to pass along to the next generation, once again, the ongoing effects of neglect and abuse.

The Guardian Parent

During my childhood, many of the adults around me often failed in their role as Guardian Parent either out of ignorance, denial, or both. Several months after confronting my parents in a letter with what had happened in our family, I visited them in person. The tension in the household was palpable. We all had so many questions, but were so afraid to speak. Tentatively and awkwardly, we began to talk. Eventually I asked my mother point-blank if she had ever suspected I was being abused. She replied yes, she did once have some very strong suspicions that Sam was molesting me. Feeling a great deal of anger, I then asked her why she had not tried to get help. To my shock, she said that she had.

Tearfully, and with great anguish, she told me the story. Although she did not have any real proof, she felt so concerned about the situation she decided she had to do something. Out of desperation she made an appointment to see a staff psychiatrist on the military base where we were stationed. When she told him of her concerns, his response was to tell her that she was simply acting like a hysterical mother. He went on to say that this type of thing simply never happened. He concluded by suggesting that she go back home and not be so obsessed about such foolish worries. I really did not want to believe what I had just heard, yet in my gut I knew my mother was telling the truth.

There are many things which need to be changed. More scientific research needs to be done addressing the psychological and physiological effects of childhood abuse in order to develop more appropriate sensitivity and treatment. The judicial system must be better educated concerning the lifelong effects of abuse and the imperative need for rigorous and consistent prosecution of perpetrators. There must be a mandate for public and private service agencies to provide treatment for the victims of childhood abuse and for community support of efforts toward prevention, detection, and education.

The Compassionate Heart of our Higher Power

It is said, in the East, that anger is very much like a hot, burning coal.[1] When we were abused as children, those who harmed us forced this searing coal into our hands. In order to cover up the truth, those who abused us used our self-protective denial against us. They convinced us to close our hands around this ember so their actions would remain hidden. They did this in several ways: coercing us into thinking that nothing happened, telling us it was our own fault, threatening us and/or others with harm, or by brainwashing us into believing what feels so wrong is good. As we come out of denial, we become aware of our pain, and recognize how we have unknowingly carried it for years. Instinctively we wish to seek out ways to return this hot coal to those who harmed us. If we eventually do find an opportunity to launch this destructive missile, we may miss our mark. Meanwhile, however, as long as we hold onto this searing ember, we are most certainly burning ourselves.

If we mistakenly blame ourselves for this pain we are doubling the harm. It is as if we are taking the white hot coal which is in our left hand, and punishing ourselves by placing it in the palm of our right hand. Our inner child needs to learn to forgive our adult selves for not listening to him in the past, or not knowing what to do for him in times of crisis. Our inner adult needs to forgive our wounded child for his self-destructive patterns of re-victimization. We can either offer up our hands to the Compassionate Heart of our Higher Power, and ask for healing, or we can continue to hold on to self-blame and self-directed rage.

During the course of my Recovery, I continued to examine how I had handled my anger and blame. With great agony, I came to realize how I had, in many ways, and at many times, made innocent others responsible for my suffering. I became aware of how often I had been out of control in my dealings with people. Acknowledging such truths is not easy. For almost my entire life I had no comprehension of these grievous errors caused by the blindness of generalized denial. With this new awareness I began, again, to work the 7th Step, once more considering the Compassionate Heart of my Higher Power. "Father, forgive me for I did not know what I was doing," is often my prayer.

The Dilemmas of the 7th Step

In reworking the 7th Step over the course of the past three years I have come upon two formidable dilemmas. The first of these was the conflict between needing to work through the anger and grief, and dealing with the problems which arise from holding onto these emotions for too long. Where is the potential for laughter and love if my heart is overwhelmed by the appropriate grief and genuine rage of my Martyred Child? While I had every right to mourn, I also wanted to get back to living. I had already lost far too many years of my precious life to the abuse, and I resented this deeply. Yet, as I continued to mourn the many losses I needed to grieve, I simply could not make the decision to just stop mourning. The past was contaminating the present and there did not seem any way to stop it. Although I knew there was more to life than I could see, everything was colored by what had happened. I desperately wanted to move beyond the grief, but how?

There was another part of myself which did not want to let go of any of the righteous anger I had for Sam. Since it is a normal and healthy part of the healing process, anger had often provided the energy which fueled the reintegration of mind, body, and spirit. Anger had also given me a sense of power, provided a much more solid sense of self, and guided me towards making those changes I needed to make. After feeling nothing for so long, feeling anything, including anger, was a welcome relief. However, in wrestling with the 7th Step, I realized it was possible I could spend the rest of my life holding onto my hate only never to find inner peace. I began to recognize how I was the one who would most certainly continue to experience the ill effects of this unreleased anger and resentment, while it would not necessarily be so for the adopted brother who abused me. Not only did I wish to be delivered from my grief, I also wanted to let go of my anger. But again, how? And if I did let go of my anger, what would continue to drive my Recovery onward?

The second dilemma I encountered while working the 7th Step was the conflict between seeking revenge and maintaining a focus upon Recovery. How could I find room in my heart today for joy and serenity if it was consumed by my desire for vengeance? I slowly began to recognize that I could not do both. My energies were finite. I could either spend my time getting on with the tasks of Recovery, or continue focusing solely upon the person who abused me. A negative relationship is still a relationship, and by seeking revenge I was still involved in a most negative relationship with Sam. Slowly I began to understand that the person who was the object of my rage no longer existed.

I slowly recognized that if I continued to carry my need for vengeance, and did not somehow release it, I was only re-victimizing my inner child. I had already done everything I could think of doing to ensure the safety of others by contacting my family and friends. Was there any point to legal charges? Who was there to sue? What else was there for me to do? As I tried to rid my mind of these thoughts, I came to face the truth that I was now hopelessly controlled by revenge. Again, stopping such thoughts was not something I could simply decide to do. Knowing you want to do something differently does not automatically tell you how. Yet, the contamination of the grief and the pain of the anger were only expanding. The fear that these feelings would never end also increased as well. Only after much searching did I happen across the solution to healing a heart filled with anger and grief, vengeance and fear: slowly, and when the time is right, you begin to get a bigger heart.

Entering into the Compassionate Heart of our Higher Power

It is difficult to make the decision to let go. I think Stephen Levine puts it well: "This is a high-wire act. To keep the heart open in hell, to maintain some loving balance in the face of all our pain and confusion. To allow life in. To heal past our fear of the unknown." [2] The conflicts at this point are often acute. The questions are real, for letting go is not just something which is accomplished with the mind, it is also done with the heart. Can I really trust my Higher Power's Compassionate Heart to heal me? If I do, how will this change me, and where will these changes lead?

By slowly nurturing the willingness to let go, the healing gently starts. As I have been able to cultivate this willingness, I have also been able to soften to the pain of the memories. At first it was as if my hand were paralyzed, still tightly clenched around the burning rage. My heart, long encrusted by denial, remained hardened and cold. But over time, by staying with this often difficult process, something gradually happened. Initially the sensation was one of a softness developing around the fist of hurt. The frozen heart began to thaw and warm. With much diligence and practice, it became easier to lean into the pain, resentment, fear, rage, and grief. While struggling with this Step, one of my Recovery Team members suggested the following technique: "Become mindful of your breathing. When you inhale, focus upon your emotions. Breath in all things, no matter how negative or dark. Be gentle, and try to feel them clearly. When you exhale, breath out only your Higher Power's compassionate love. Visualize the gift of His healing light surrounding the hurt and pain. Trust that this light has been with you throughout your entire life."

At times as I have followed this technique, there have been many intense emotional reactions, as well as powerful physical sensations. My heart literally seemed to be breaking, expanding, even exploding within my chest. The tears flowed freely. When these reactions were most extreme I would become frightened. I tried to remind myself that if the abuse did not kill me then, the healing would not kill me now. Oddly, at other times I would even find myself laughing out loud in sheer relief.

The pain has not gone away as I first had imagined it would when I began working the 7th Step. Rather, it has been transformed. It is now something which can be worked with as it arises. There is something bigger than the past, the infinitely Compassionate Heart of my Higher Power. In my mind forgiveness does not equal re-entering denial. Forgiveness means allowing the memories to remain but not actively holding onto, and being controlled by, the pain. I am beginning to recognize Recovery need not be fueled by anger alone, for I am slowly letting it go. Instead, the new source of healing can be love.

As my Recovery has continued, I have begun to see other things which I had not recognized before. In his book *When Bad Things Happen to Good People* Rabbi Harold Kushner writes, "When we are stunned by some tragedy, we can only see and feel the tragedy. Only with time and distance can we see the tragedy in the context of a whole life and a whole world."[3] The abuse I suffered did not occur in a vacuum. It happened in a family whose history is probably not all that different from the history of many other families. With an awakened compassion comes the potential for understanding.

> **The softest thing in the universe**
> **Overcomes the hardest thing in the universe.**
> **That without substance can enter**
> **where there is no room.**
>
> **Teaching without words and work without doing**
> **are understood by very few.**
>
> — *Lao Tsu*
> from the *Tao Te Ching*

Exercises for the 7th Step

Due to the generalized effects of denial, we survivors are often unaware of our feelings, or where these feelings tend to become centered or located in our bodies. The goal of the first group of exercises is to help us to begin to become aware of these sensations. Once aware of them we can begin to discern between the positive aspects of these feelings and those which are negative. The second set of exercises is designed to help us begin to work with these emotions as we consider the Compassionate Heart of our Higher Power.

Part I — Becoming Aware of our Feelings

1. When I become aware of physical pain, what parts of my body tend to hurt most?

___ face or forehead	___ jaw
___ back of head	___ neck
___ shoulders	___ upper arms
___ elbows	___ lower arms
___ wrists	___ hands
___ fingers	___ upper back
___ mid-back	___ lower back
___ chest or heart	___ stomach
___ diaphragm	___ colon or belly
___ pelvic region	___ hips
___ thighs	___ knees
___ ankles	___ feet or toes

Which of the following words best describes the type of pain I typically experience:

___ acute	___ aching	___ chronic
___ dull	___ numb	___ piercing
___ pinched	___ sharp	___ sore
___ stabbing	___ stinging	___ tender
___ throbbing	___ tingling	___ twinging

2. When I become aware of anger, where in my body do I first notice this sensation?

___ face or forehead	___ jaw
___ back of head	___ neck
___ shoulders	___ upper arms
___ elbows	___ lower arms
___ wrists	___ hands
___ fingers	___ upper back
___ mid-back	___ lower back
___ chest or heart	___ stomach
___ diaphragm	___ colon or belly
___ pelvic region	___ hips
___ thighs	___ knees
___ ankles	___ feet or toes

Which of the following words best describes for me how positive anger feels:

___ committed   ___ decisive   ___ dedicated
___ determined   ___ firm   ___ focused
___ powerful   ___ resolute   ___ solid
___ steadfast   ___ strong   ___ tenacious

Which of the following words best describes for me how negative anger feels:

___ brutal   ___ callous   ___ cold
___ cruel   ___ frozen   ___ harsh
___ hot   ___ obsessive   ___ rigid
___ stern   ___ tense   ___ violent

3. When I become aware of fear, where in my body do I first notice this sensation?

___ face or forehead   ___ jaw
___ back of head   ___ neck
___ shoulders   ___ upper arms
___ elbows   ___ lower arms
___ wrists   ___ hands
___ fingers   ___ upper back
___ mid-back   ___ lower back
___ chest or heart   ___ stomach
___ diaphragm   ___ colon or belly
___ pelvic region   ___ hips
___ thighs   ___ knees
___ ankles   ___ feet or toes

Which of the following words best describes for me how positive fear feels:

___ alert   ___ careful   ___ cautious
___ concerned   ___ guarded   ___ heedful
___ prudent   ___ restrained   ___ safe
___ vigilant   ___ wary   ___ watchful

Which of the following words best describes for me how negative fear feels:

___ cold   ___ crippled   ___ disabled
___ helpless   ___ impotent   ___ frightened
___ paralyzed   ___ paranoid   ___ powerless
___ scared   ___ terrified   ___ worried

4. When I become aware of resentment, where in my body do I first notice this sensation?

___ face or forehead   ___ jaw

___ back of head	___ neck
___ shoulders	___ upper arms
___ elbows	___ lower arms
___ wrists	___ hands
___ fingers	___ upper back
___ mid-back	___ lower back
___ chest or heart	___ stomach
___ diaphragm	___ colon or belly
___ pelvic region	___ hips
___ thighs	___ knees
___ ankles	___ feet or toes

Which of the following words best describes for me how unresolved resentment feels:

___ bitter	___ burning	___ caustic
___ cold	___ corrosive	___ dark
___ dirty	___ flat	___ frigid
___ gloomy	___ hard	___ heavy
___ hot	___ lifeless	___ painful
___ restricted	___ stiff	___ throbbing
___ tight	___ unclean	___ upsetting

5. In my family of origin, which of the following were present (or do I suspect were present) within the past two, three, or four generations?

___ problems with alcohol	___ problems with drugs
___ emotional neglect/abuse	___ physical neglect/abuse
___ sexual abuse	___ childhood abandonment
___ religious fanaticism	___ mental illness
___ chronic physical illness	___ premature death
___ chronic marital discord	___ divorce or separation
___ suicide	___ work addiction

___ legal problems or imprisonment
___ war or military conflict
___ political revolution or political upheaval
___ drastic social change or upheaval
___ poverty or economic reversal

Other family traumas, problems or secrets:

A. _____

_____

B. _____

_____

Part II — Working with our Emotions

1. Take a few moments to review the exercises just completed. Before beginning this second set of 12 Step Journal Exercises, try to think about which of the following emotions in its negative form would be the easiest to work on, and which one would be the most difficult. If you wish, rank them all on a scale from one (the easiest) to four (the hardest) to help you make this decision.

___ Pain   ___ Anger   ___ Fear   ___ Resentment

As your Recovery continues and you begin to rework the 7th Step at a later time, you might think about using some of these same, following strategies for working with the second most difficult emotion on your list. Consider sharing these exercises with your Recovery Team for their ideas and suggestions.

2. What color or colors do I find to be the most comforting and soothing?

___ gray   ___ white   ___ yellow   ___ orange
___ red   ___ brown   ___ green   ___ blue
___ pink   ___ purple   ___ black
___ gold   ___ silver

3. Do I have any clothes or personal belongings that are these colors?

Yes ___ No ___
If yes, what are they?
A. _____
B. _____

If I do not have any clothes or personal belongings that are these colors, what would be the things I would like to get or make for myself which would be these colors? (Be as creative as you want to be!)

A. _____
B. _____

4. Which of the following images might help me to picture in the mind's eye my Higher Power's compassion?

___ warm water   ___ cool water
___ bright light   ___ soft light
___ warm air or breezes   ___ cool air or breezes
___ warm cloth or blanket   ___ cool cloth or blanket
___ warm mist or cloud   ___ cool mist or cloud

Other healing images:

A. _____

_____

B. _____

_____

5. Think back to a place and time when you felt accepted and loved unconditionally. Take a few moments now to describe that place and time along with those feelings of acceptance and love.

_____
_____
_____
_____
_____
_____
_____
_____

6. Now, try to think back to a place and time when you felt the most peaceful and serene. Again, take a few moments to describe that place and time along with those feelings of peacefulness and serenity.

_____
_____
_____
_____
_____
_____
_____
_____

7. The next time I become aware of a negative sensation in my body, I can try one or more of the following strategies for working with it. (Please check those which you think may best work for you.)

_____ The next time I find myself becoming aware of this negative feeling, I will focus upon my breathing. When I inhale, I will let myself really feel this emotion. When I breathe out, I will exhale the opposite of this emotion. An example for Fear would be breathing in "scared" and exhaling "calm."

_____ The next time I find myself becoming aware of this negative feeling, I will make sure to wear one of my healing colors, or that I have this color somewhere in the room with me.

_____ The next time I become aware of this negative feeling I will not ignore it. Instead, I will go to a quiet place and be alone, and in the mind's eye picture this negative feeling being surrounded by a healing image of my Higher Power's compassion and love.

_____ The next time I become aware of this negative feeling I will not deny its presence. Instead, I will be alone for a while with this feeling, and imagine with the mind's eye that I am taking this emotion with me to a place where I have felt at peace in the past.

Step 8

◆
───────────────────────────

Specifying Offenses

We make a list of all persons we may have harmed as a result of our having been abused. We become willing to make amends to them all.

Childhood abuse caused chaos in our lives and we may have unwittingly harmed others. Naming those to whom we may owe amends is one way of addressing our personal pandemonium. The 8th Step is a means by which we can begin to move toward serenity and sanity. The false guilt or shame of our wounded child can feel just as real as the honest contrition of our adult selves. Differences between false guilt and genuine remorse or unwarranted shame and healthy accountability are extremely important and must be discerned with care. With the stage set in childhood, it is likely we carried a confused perception of responsibility into our adult lives.

It takes courage to search our past as we work this Step. Yet, by developing the willingness to name those we may have offended, we continue to challenge the denial which has controlled us. Without realizing it at the time, we most likely harmed ourselves when we were out of control. We make amends for the sake of those we have hurt, and also for ourselves. The following section focuses upon the two primary sources of offenses against ourselves and others: **dependent relationships** and **patterns of revictimization**.

Dependent Relationships

Victimized individuals tend to attract, and be attracted to, other wounded persons. Statistically it is quite likely some (or even most) of the people in our present lives were themselves victims of some form of abuse or neglect. If they are in denial, and have not yet begun their own Recovery, we may then be trapped in a dangerous cycle without knowing it! Someone who is lonely or scared may look to us for rescue from these disturbing feelings. Without thinking, they may blame us when they experience hurt or disappointment. If they convince us that we are the cause of their agony, then we are in very deep trouble indeed. Out of erroneous guilt and shame, we attempt to heal them or alter their situations. Not having reached the point in our Recovery where we can mindfully consider and vigorously challenge such claims, we automatically fall into the trap of unfounded and misplaced responsibility.

Such patterns, called by some *co-dependent behavior*, are always circular and only worsen until actively broken.[1] Emotionally, we are totally powerless to change things for others. They may have given us all the responsibility for their well-being, but, in truth, we have absolutely no authority at all in this matter! Several writers have focused upon how women become entrapped in such relationships; however, I suspect dependency among males is just as prevalent, although expressed somewhat differently.[2] As you consider the 8th Step, ask yourself the following questions: Am I still taking on the false responsibility for someone else's Recovery? In what ways am I trying to do the 12 Steps for them? Am I trying to be their Higher Power? Just because someone proclaims you to be his or her savior, does not necessarily make it so.

The other side of this dependency dance is when we are in pain and blame others. As children this was true, for the adults in our lives did have power over us and were responsible when we experienced pain. However, we could still be trapped by the false perception that other people can supply us with inner harmony. When these people threaten to abandon us, we react with panic. In terror and desperation we promise to do anything to keep them in our lives.

In relationships based upon fear and avoidance, there is little room for unconditional love and gentle patience, true giving and shared joy. Instead, such unions are characterized by anger, hurt, resentment, and anxiety. As the partners withdraw from each other, drug or alcohol abuse often increases. Sexuality may begin to take on manipulative, escapist, or even assaultive qualities. Preexisting emotional problems typically worsen, and character defects intensify. Interactions become caustic, critical, sarcastic or abusive. In these enmeshed liaisons it is almost impossible to tell where one person ends and the other begins. A certain disaster is when you have two out-of-control adults, each certain of their own impending doom, hopelessly bound together.

Patterns of Re-victimization

Before Recovery we may have acted out the role of victim and allowed others to exploit us, thus causing additional injury. We may have mistreated others in the same ways we were wronged. Some of us may have unconsciously assumed the role of both victim and victimizer at various times in our dealings with others. If the lessons we learned about relationships were those taught through abuse, we may have the erroneous idea that intimacy and sexuality are one and the same, or that brutality and love are somehow intertwined. Having never been shown any appropriate models of positive control and healthy self-discipline, we may have fallen prey to giving in to all impulses.

We may have been coerced into believing that compliance amounts to giving affection. Repeatedly we were shown how to accept anger and abuse as a form of attention. Love has always hurt and felt confusing. While we may not have deliberately asked for these things to happen, neither did we know how to actively challenge this pattern of revictimization. The following is not intended as a comprehensive listing of all offenses possible. Instead, it is offered as a beginning point to help free us from our circular life patterns.

Possible Offenses in the Six Life Areas

Psychological

Offenses to Others
Misplaced anger
Misplaced blame
Verbal abuse
Mental control/manipulation

Offenses to Self
Self-directed anger
Self-directed blame
Excessive self-criticism
Avoiding treatment

Spiritual

Offenses to Others
Spiritual discrimination
Displacing anger on Church
Displacing blame on Church
Expecting others to
    be our Higher Power

Offenses to Self
Little or no self-forgiveness
Little or no self-compassion
Compulsive religious or
    ritualistic behaviors
Avoidance of spiritual issues

Sexual

Offenses to Others
Unsafe sex
Voyeurism
Sadistic behaviors
Rape/other sexual assault
    involving adults
Sex with children

Offenses to Self
Unsafe sex
Compulsive sexual behaviors
Masochistic behaviors
Sexual re-victimization
Prostitution

Physical

Offenses to Others
Physical violence
Spouse/partner/child abuse
Assault with a vehicle or
    weapon
Drug dealing
Murder

Offenses to Self
Drug or alcohol abuse
Self-mutilation
Suicide attempts
Eating disorders
Avoiding health care
Excessive or compulsive exercise

Social

Offenses to Others
Dependent relationships
Racial discrimination
Sexual discrimination
Social prejudice
Neglect of children

Offenses to Self
Avoidance of relationships
Avoidance of intimacy
Remaining in bad relationships
Remaining in victim role
Avoidance of time alone

Economic

Offenses to Others	*Offenses to Self*
Bad checks	Lack of household budget
Old or unpaid debts	Lack of Recovery budget
Theft	No savings account
Fraud	No retirement account
Bankruptcy	Compulsive spending

Exercises for the 8th Step

There are at least three options available which may be helpful when working this Step in your 12 Step Journal.

Option I is to write down today's date along with the name or initials of those you feel you may have offended. You do not have to put down your reasons for adding this person to the list. Sometimes when people begin to work this Step for the first time they may not know how they may have offended someone, or why they feel the need to make amends; they just know that they do. Another reason for not specifying offenses on paper may be a realistic fear of someone reading your Recovery Journal. Please do not try to decide if you really need to make amends or not to these people for now. That particular issue will be explored more fully in the 9th Step.

Option II for working the 8th Step is again to include today's date along with the name or the initials of the person you feel you may have harmed. However, this time the list is broken down into each of the six Life Areas, and a section has been added for you to note how you feel you have offended or harmed that individual. Within the space provided, try to be as specific as possible in outlining this offense in terms of who, what, where, when, and how. This may not be easy to do but, if you choose to use this option, try to be as honest as possible. You are also asked to rank how difficult you think it would be to make amends for this particular offense. As you work and rework the 12 Steps you may find yourself adding names to or removing names from these lists, which is an indication of your increasing abilities of courageous discernment and evolving wisdom.

Option III explores those offenses which we may have committed against ourselves within the six Life Areas. Again a space is provided for today's date along with a section for you to specify the manner in which you may have harmed yourself in the past. Try to be as specific as possible. As before in the previous exercise, there is a place for you to rank how difficult you feel it would be to make amends to yourself for this offense.

Option I — Specifying Offenses In General

The purpose of this section is to list only the names, or initials, of those you feel you may have offended. Note in the space provided the day you add a particular person to this list. This will be helpful when working the 9th Step. If you choose this Option, please do not write down the specifics of your offenses. When you have completed this list, no matter how brief, please then rank these amends to be made from the one you feel would be the easiest (number 1) to the most difficult (number 2, number 3, etc.).

Name	Date	Rank
A. _____	_____	____
B. _____	_____	____
C. _____	_____	____
D. _____	_____	____

Option II - Specifying Offenses against Others

Psychological

Date _____ Name _____ Rank _____

The reason I feel the need to make amends to this person is

_____

_____

I feel that making amends for this offense would be

     painful   very hard   challenging   fairly easy   very easy

     10++++++9+++++8+++++7+++++6+++++5++++4+++++3+++++2+++++1

Spiritual

Date _____ Name _____ Rank _____

The reason I feel the need to make amends to this person is

_____

_____

I feel that making amends for this offense would be

     painful   very hard   challenging   fairly easy   very easy

     10++++++9+++++8+++++7+++++6+++++5++++4+++++3+++++2+++++1

Sexual

Date _____ Name _____ Rank _____

The reason I feel the need to make amends to this person is

_____

_____

I feel that making amends for this offense would be

     painful   very hard   challenging   fairly easy   very easy

     10++++++9+++++8+++++7+++++6+++++5++++4+++++3+++++2+++++1

Physical

Date _____ Name _____ Rank _____

The reason I feel the need to make amends to this person is

_____

_____

I feel that making amends for this offense would be

     painful   very hard   challenging   fairly easy   very easy

     10++++++9+++++8+++++7+++++6+++++5++++4+++++3+++++2+++++1

Social

Date _____ Name _____ Rank _____

The reason I feel the need to make amends to this person is

_____

_____

I feel that making amends for this offense would be

     painful   very hard   challenging   fairly easy   very easy

     10+++++9+++++8+++++7+++++6+++++5++++4+++++3+++++2+++++1

Economic

Date _____ Name _____ Rank _____

The reason I feel the need to make amends to this person is

_____

_____

I feel that making amends for this offense would be

     painful   very hard   challenging   fairly easy   very easy

     10+++++9+++++8+++++7+++++6+++++5++++4+++++3+++++2+++++1

Option III — Specifying Offenses against Self

Psychological

Date _____ Name _____ Rank _____

The reason I feel the need to make amends to myself is

_____

_____

I feel that making amends for this offense would be

     painful   very hard   challenging   fairly easy   very easy

     10+++++9+++++8+++++7+++++6+++++5++++4+++++3+++++2+++++1

Spiritual

Date _____ Name _____ Rank _____

The reason I feel the need to make amends to myself is

_____

_____

I feel that making amends for this offense would be

     painful   very hard   challenging   fairly easy   very easy

     10+++++9+++++8+++++7+++++6+++++5++++4+++++3+++++2+++++1

Sexual

Date _____ Name _____ Rank _____

The reason I feel the need to make amends to myself is

_____

_____

I feel that making amends for this offense would be

     painful   very hard   challenging   fairly easy   very easy

     10+++++9+++++8+++++7+++++6+++++5++++4+++++3+++++2+++++1

Physical

Date _____ Name _____ Rank _____

The reason I feel the need to make amends to myelf is

_____

_____

I feel that making amends for this offense would be

     painful   very hard   challenging   fairly easy   very easy

     10+++++9+++++8+++++7+++++6+++++5++++4+++++3+++++2+++++1

Social
Date _____ Name _____ Rank _____
The reason I feel the need to make amends to myself is

_____

_____

I feel that making amends for this offense would be
      painful   very hard   challenging   fairly easy   very easy
      10+++++9+++++8+++++7+++++6+++++5++++4+++++3+++++2+++++1

Economic
Date _____ Name _____ Rank _____
The reason I feel the need to make amends to myself is

_____

_____

I feel that making amends for this offense would be
      painful   very hard   challenging   fairly easy   very easy
      10+++++9+++++8+++++7+++++6+++++5++++4+++++3+++++2+++++1

Step 9

◆

Making Amends

We make amends to those persons we have harmed or victimized, except when to do so would injure them, others, or ourselves. We also make amends to ourselves.

The phrase "to make amends" can be defined several ways. If the harm done was physical, then compensation may need to be made, if possible, in a tangible manner. If the transgression was social and involves specific shortcomings, the atonement might then be aimed at healing this wounded relationship. To make amends also means to remove faults or reform our thinking in order to avoid making the same mistakes again.

It may be rather easy to make amends, especially when the offenses are obvious and the amends themselves do not cause additional problems. However, it is much more unsettling to face those difficult amends where we have obviously caused serious harm to another human being. In some situations we run the risk of having our motives misunderstood, or having our efforts rejected outright. Since we cannot predict nor control how others will react to our offers, our fears may be quite valid.

No one expects us to complete this Step within any specific time frame for there are no absolute deadlines. In working and reworking the 9th Step, we naturally add and remove amends from our lists. Also, the amends we eventually choose to make may be quite different from those originally planned. By beginning to make amends for past offenses we discover we are no longer running in fear from those people we may have offended. Rather, we will begin to walk toward them with self-confidence, offering the same gifts of renewal first given us through our Higher Power.

Before actually attempting to make amends, please review your plans with at least one member of your Recovery Team. It is extremely important to accurately discern between those whom you have truly offended, and those whom you have not. The remaining sections of this chapter offer suggested guidelines for making amends to others and to yourself. For both of these the format is the same. First, each topic in the exercises is discussed and then followed by the exercises themselves. Feel free to modify these exercises to meet your individual needs as you work them within your 12 Step Recovery Journal.

Exercises For The 9th Step
Making Amends To Others

Part I - Analyzing The Amends: Points To Remember

Point 1. In the 8th Step you were asked to rank those amends you feel you need to make from the easiest to the most difficult. Starting with the easiest and working your way up to the most difficult is one method of gaining experience in making successful amends. If you begin first with the most difficult amends on the list you could be setting yourself up for failure. **The only time I would recommend you not follow this ranking is if you are involved in any behavior which threatens the life or health of yourself or others. Such actions include physical violence, unsafe sex, drunk driving, drug dealing, neglect of children, self-mutilation and sexual abuse. If you are involved in any such activity, I strongly suggest that you contact one of your Recovery Team members at once for immediate help and intervention!**

While it is important to identify those whom we may have harmed, it is also helpful to write down the date we first became aware of the need to make amends to that person. Doing so will aid us as we keep track of the time frame we will set for ourselves in working this Step. While writing out the specifics of the offense may not be easy, it is necessary in order for our Recovery Team to help us plan more meaningful amends.

Point 2. Often, in the rush to move on with their Recovery, people mistakenly feel they have to make amends for past offenses all at once. However, going too fast only creates problems in addition to those which already exist. Setting aside a realistic and cautious amount of time to work through one specific amends at a time increases the probability of success with this amends and those which follow.

Point 3. As we analyze this proposed amends, it is important to obtain insights and comments from our Recovery Team. Again, we are beginning to learn to make amends and in this case the old cliché of two (or even three) heads being better than one definitely applies. Noting the dates we have discussed the upcoming amends helps to maintain our focus and encourages us not to move too hastily.

Point 4. When we have set time limits, consulted our Recovery Team, and specified the offense, we can begin to give thought to our expectations in making this amends. If we do not clarify our own expectations we may be jeopardizing our success. By giving this situation some serious thought, we eventually reach the goal of a positive amends and avoid unnecessary disappointment.

Point 5. Since much behavior is learned and/or imitated, it is a good idea to think about who taught us and how we learned these behaviors. While this does not free us from responsibility, it softens the harshness of self-criticism to know we may have done these things simply because we did not know any better.

Point 6. We had models for negative or dysfunctional behavior. Now it is important to consider persons who can offer examples for making good amends as well as positive alternative behaviors. As such healthy role models come to mind write their names down on the list.

Point 7. There is an extremely fine line between doing something for someone and doing something to them. The most common mistake made when attempting amends is the failure to ask the person what it is they want. By telling the other person exactly what you want, and requesting they tell you exactly what they need, you are setting up a situation where everybody wins. Do not assume what you have planned to do is in fact something they want to have done for them, or to them. There may be situations when you offer amends but the person involved either does not feel you have offended them (therefore do not need amends) or they are unwilling to accept the amends. In either case, forcing an amends upon another person is unwise.

It is easy to confuse making amends with giving a gift. Gifts are given with no expectations at all, whereas amends are made with the expectation of healing the relationship. Making amends under the guise of giving a gift never works and leaves both parties unsatisfied.

Part II - Planning the Amends
Point 1. This section is simply a place to brainstorm. Give yourself permission to be creative when writing out ways to make amends. It helps if you do not reject any idea, no matter how unusual or outlandish. Allow yourself as much time as possible and use as much paper as necessary to write out these ideas.

Point 2. Once you have generated a list of possible amends, you can go back and look at this list with a more critical eye. You might think about sharing this list with your Recovery Team for their comments. Which ones are likely to succeed? Which ones are likely to fail?

Point 3. For many people the concept of a Win-Win situation sounds very strange and feels extremely foreign. As children we were very familiar with Win-Lose arrangements. The abusers won, we lost. Without realizing it, we may have fallen into the trap of believing that all relationships and interactions must follow this pattern. This is not true. While Win-Win arrangements do require more thought, creativity and work than confrontations, such arrangements can be found.

In order for the amends being contemplated to benefit both yourself and the person offended (Win-Win), I feel some rather specific criteria must be met: 1) we have asked the person how to make amends; 2) the amends itself does not endanger our lives or the lives of others; 3) the amends does not threaten our Recovery, and 4) the amends will not create more problems. Before committing yourself to any plan for making amends be sure to get the opinion of your Recovery Team.

Point 4. Murphy's Law of Recovery states, "If something can go wrong when making amends, it probably will." If something serious could happen while making this amends, consider having at least one witness present.

Part III - Final Plans for Making Amends

In this section all prior work is collected together and given one final examination. The amends is specified, and a target date is set. Expectations have been noted, risks detailed, and Win-Win guidelines have been confirmed. You have discussed this amends with your Recovery Team and have negotiated the means by which you are to make amends. You have also given yourself time to think about this amends and have not rushed into it.

Taking any risk naturally causes anxiety. Making amends is risky for no other reason than that we have little or no experience in thinking or acting in this manner. It is not unusual for individuals, when actually making amends, to experience a number of intense emotions. However, if you begin to feel strangely uncomfortable about any aspect of this amends, please listen to these intuitions. This gut feeling may be there for a good reason. You do not have to complete this amends at this time if you do not feel good about it. You can always come back to this situation later.

Part IV - Lessons Learned from Making Amends

After you have made an amends it is important to be able to recognize what worked and what did not work. Taking time to review these questions with your Recovery Team may be a most wise investment in your ongoing healing.

Making Amends to Others

Part I — Analyzing the Amends

1. Date Offense Noted _____
Name of person who was offended _____
Life Area in which offense was committed _____
I feel the need to make amends to this person because

_____

_____

2. Before I attempt to make amends I will wait
___ 30 days   ___ 60 days   ___ 90 days
___ 4 months   ___ 6 months   ___ 1 year

3. Before I attempt to make amends I will discuss this matter at least two times
with the following Recovery Team member for his/her guidance:
Recovery Team member _____
Dates amends discussed:
Session Number 1: _____ Session Number 2: _____
Session Number 3: _____ Session Number 4: _____
When we talked about the amends for this offense, his/her comments and
suggestions were _____

_____

_____

4. What are my hopes and expectations in making amends to this person?
A._____
B. _____

5. In looking back at this offense, who were the people who taught me to treat
others in this manner? Who were my role models for this behavior? (You may
use titles, names, or initials.)
A._____
B. _____

6. Is there anyone in my life now who might be a positive role model for me in
handling this situation in a healthy manner?
A._____
B. _____

7. When I asked the person I felt I had offended about how I could make amends to them, he/she said _____

_____

_____

_____

Part II — Planning the Amends

1. My ideas for making amends to this person are:

A._____

B. _____

C. _____

2. Of the ideas above, which one is most likely to succeed? (Please circle the appropriate letter.)

Of the ideas above, which one is most likely to fail? (Please cross out the appropriate letter.)

3. Does my plan meet the following Win-Win Guidelines for Making Amends?

_____ Yes _____ No   I have asked the person I may have offended how I can make amends.

_____ Yes _____ No   This plan is safe and does not endanger my life or the lives of others.

_____ Yes _____ No   This plan is realistic and does not threaten my Recovery.

_____ Yes _____ No   This plan is positive and will not cause me any undue problems in other Life Areas.

4. In making amends for this offense, what might go wrong?

A._____

B. _____

C._____

Part III - Final Plans for Making Amends

The person I will make amends to is _____

The target date for making amends is _____

This amends is in the_____ Life Area.

I have talked this matter over with a Recovery Team member.

Yes _____ No _____

I followed my self-determined waiting period before making this amends.
____ Yes ____ No

My expectations for making this amends are:

    A._____

    B. _____

My plans for making this amends are:

What I will do _____

When I will do it _____

Where I will do it _____

How I will do it _____

How many of the Win-Win guidelines for making amends does this plan meet? (please circle)

    All 4   3 out of 4   2 out of 4   1 out of 4   None

This plan involves the following risks:

    A._____

    B. _____

Optional - I will have the following person(s) present as witness(es) when I make this amends:

    A._____

    B. _____

Part IV — Lessons Learned from This Amends

If I had the opportunity to do this amends again, what would I have done differently?

    A._____

    B. _____

If I had the opportunity to do this amends again, what would I have done the same?

    A._____

    B. _____

What lessons have I learned from making this amends?

    A._____

    B. _____

Making Amends to Yourself

Points 1 and 2. In reviewing the list of offenses against yourself compiled in the 8th Step, please examine them in terms of difficulty. As in the section on Making Amends To Others, you might think about starting with those amends which are the easiest to make. **The only time I feel you should ignore this ranking is if you are involved in any activity which is a direct threat to your well-being. If this is the case, please contact one of your Recovery Team members at once for immediate help!**

In this section please note the date you became aware of this offense so you will be able to monitor change and affirm progress. Space is also provided to write out as best you can the specific ways you have offended or harmed yourself. By clearly detailing these errors, your Recovery Team will have a better idea of how they can be helpful. Again, a target date helps to keep your Recovery efforts on track.

Point 3. Your Recovery Team can be a vital resource as you begin to make amends to yourself. They can help you to think about yourself in new ways. Under their guidance you can experiment with new thoughts and perspectives. When things go well, they are there to encourage you. When things do not go as planned, they will be able to help you discern the reasons why your attempts were less than successful.

Point 4. As children, we had someone outside us who modeled these same words, attitudes or behaviors and we unknowingly internalized them, thus making them a part of ourselves. By becoming aware of those negative thoughts or self-defeating behaviors we learned from others, we can replace such patterns with new ones.

Point 5. By affirming our right to treat ourselves with patience and kindness, we further open the door to Recovery. The list of possibilities for self-amends included within this 9th Step exercise is only a short outline. Please consider reviewing the list with your Recovery Team. Give yourself permission to generate your own list of potential amends, and feel free to add these new ideas for self-amends in the space provided. Give to yourself the same positive amends which you would so readily make to others.

Exercises for the 9th Step
Making Amends to Yourself

1. Date Offense Against Self Noted _____
Life Area in which I harmed myself _____
I feel the need to make amends to myself because

_____
_____

2. I will attempt to begin making amends to myself for this offense within the next

___ 2 weeks   ___ 3 weeks   ___ 4 weeks
___ 2 months   ___ 3 months   ___ 6 months

3. I will talk with the following Recovery Team member about how I can begin to make amends to myself:
Recovery Team Member _____
When we talked about amends to myself, his/her comments and suggestions were _____

_____
_____

4. Who taught me to treat myself this way? (You may use titles, names, or initials.)

A._____
B._____

5. What things can I do now to make amends to myself? (You may check more than one.)

_____ Practice having some compassion for myself because I was out of control and had not yet entered Recovery.
_____ Begin to forgive myself for the past.
_____ Remain committed to my Recovery.
_____ Dedicate myself to working the remaining 12 Steps.
_____ Practice seeing myself through the forgiving and loving eyes of my Higher Power.
_____ Write a letter of amends to myself in my 12 Step Recovery Journal.
_____ Pray for myself.
_____ Ask a Recovery Team Member to pray for me.
_____ Make a commitment for the next 4 months to work on stopping this

behavior with the help of my Recovery Team and my Higher Power.

_____ Make a commitment for the next 6 months to finding another way of handling my problems with the help of my Recovery Team and my Higher Power.

Other possible amends to self:

A._____

B._____

Step 10

$\blacklozenge$

Daily Growth

We continue to take a daily personal inventory, and when we have been in error we promptly admit it.

We adult survivors had to become experts at denial in order to survive. However, this denial now causes our lives to be out of control in many subtle and not so subtle ways. The title of Gerald Jampolski's book *Love Is Letting Go Of Fear* sums up this phase of our Recovery, as fear is a root source of our denial. In taking a Daily Inventory, we decontaminate our lives of this fear by separating past fears from present realities. We often stumble at first but we keep at it. Like most things in life, practice helps.

Daily Inventory is not meant to be a form of brutal self-criticism or harsh judgment. Instead it is a tool to help us build a gentle awareness or mindfulness of our thoughts, feelings, actions and choices. We begin to recognize things which do or do not work for us the next time we find ourselves in a similar situation. It is extremely important we improve our ability to know what we are really thinking and feeling. Sometimes survivors have extraordinary delay between events in their lives and awareness of emotional reaction. Consider using the Daily Inventory as a deliberate, disciplined, day-to-day Reality Check.

We adult survivors in Recovery are sometimes not the easiest people in the world to live with. This is especially true if we are checking out, having flashbacks, grieving our losses, yo-yoing through mood swings or simply trying to figure out how to be truly genuine with our feelings. For example, you tell a friend or your partner three weeks after the fact that you resent their having told you what to do rather than asking you. They will probably either discount your reactions, or they will not be able to see how your complaints are relevant, because they forgot about this incident a long time ago. While your point is quite valid, they just do not understand what that old piece of business has to do with the here and now. Turn the situation around, put yourself in their shoes, and I think you will see what I mean.

A suggested outline for structured Daily Inventory has been included and each of the questions listed will be examined. Again, there is no right or wrong way of taking the 10th Step so only consider those questions which apply to your own unique Recovery.

Exploring the Daily Inventory

Points 1 and 2. Awareness of Stress

One important reason to keep a Daily Inventory concerns the paradoxical nature of Recovery itself. When under stress, we humans tend to fall back onto those coping skills which are safe, easy, and familiar. In Recovery we are deliberately trying to learn to do things in new ways and actively challenge our old life patterns. Combine the stress of conscious, healthy change with this tendency to fall into old habits when under stress, and you have one of the great paradoxes of Recovery: the very process increases the probability of relapsing into dysfunctional coping skills!

There are some indicators which help us become aware of this stress: sleep patterns, coffee or tea consumption, how much we smoke, muscle tension, use of other stimulants or tranquilizers, eating patterns, and our general level of anxiety. By becoming mindful of these indicators, we can make needed adjustments and begin to take better care of ourselves.

Point 3. False Responsibility

By using our Daily Inventory, we can think more critically when others assert we are responsible for their negative reactions or irrational behaviors.

We tend to feel pretty good about ourselves when someone says "You make me so happy!" It's a trap...Go back! We in Recovery need no longer assume someone is automatically right just because he or she says we have done something to them, or for them. We begin to see we are not another's Higher Power.

Point 4. Recognizing Resentments

Denying the reality of resentment does not work anywhere. Saving up and unloading all at once does not work either. If we can take resentments back to where they belong, it is unlikely that we will dump them elsewhere. By becoming aware of our resentments we will find it more difficult to allow the past to interfere with the present.

Point 5. Releasing Resentment

Just because we are aware of resentment does not automatically tell us what to do about it, but we should try not to give up too soon. As in the 9th Step on Making Amends, creativity can be a powerful resource. If after you give the situation some thought and do not come up with a workable solution, you may want to consider the resources of your Recovery Team.

Point 6. Recognizing Dependencies

Our unrealistic expectations of others can set us up when they fail to meet our needs or make us happy. As we continue our Daily Inventory, we will begin to challenge these unrealistic expectations of people.

Points 7 and 8. Displaced Anger and Making Amends

In the past we were not allowed to feel or express our resentments, so we did not learn how to handle them appropriately. Now we are aware of this pattern; we can take responsibility for our behavior and make positive changes. We may not have a great deal of experience in making amends, so exploring options with our Recovery Team may prove helpful.

Points 9 and 10. Affirmations and Goals

Sometimes, when things go well for us, we tend to think this happened by sheer accident. However, there are usually specific things we do, or choose not to do, that help us to meet our goals. We are doing something that works! In the 6th Step, we explored our need to affirm the truth about our rights as individuals and how to make these affirmations concrete.

By working our Daily Inventory, we begin to validate our successes and learn from our errors. As we take a few moments to consider the information we have gathered through this gentle examination of ourselves, we can begin to **think** about our goals and **choose** how to reach them. The simple act of selecting tomorrow's Affirmation and Goal is a powerful means of challenging our past hopelessness.

Exercises for the Daily Inventory - 10th Step

1. How high or low were my external stress levels today?

       Extremely High   High Moderate Low Extremely Low

       10   9   8   7   6   5   4   3   2   1   0

How high or low were my internal emotional and psychological stress levels today?

       Extremely High   High Moderate Low Extremely Low

       10   9   8   7   6   5   4   3   2   1   0

How well did I sleep last night?

       Not at all   About average   Very Well

       10   9   8   7   6   5   4   3   2   1   0

How much food did I eat today?

       Binge eating   Too much Average Too little None at all

       10   9   8   7   6   5   4   3   2   1   0

Did I drink more coffee or tea than usual today?

       Yes ___ No ___

Did I smoke more cigarettes than usual today?

       Yes ___ No ___

Was my use of other stimulants higher than usual today?

       Yes ___ No ___

Was my use of other tranquilizers higher than usual today?

       Yes ___ No ___

2. Which of my muscles are most tense?

       A. _____

       B. _____

Which of my muscles are most relaxed?

       A. _____

       B. _____

At this moment, my overall anxiety level is:

       Extremely High   High Moderate Low Extremely Low

       10   9   8   7   6   5   4   3   2   1   0

3. Did someone else try to make me responsible for his/her Serenity this day?

       Yes ___ No ___

If yes, who? _____

How did he/she try to make me responsible for his/her Serenity?

_____

_____

_____

4. Do I have any resentment about what happened today?

      Yes ___ No ___

If yes, is it against a person or thing?

The person I resent is _____

and I resent him/her because _____

_____

The thing I resent is _____

and I resent this thing because _____

_____

5. Can I think of a way to address this resentment?

      Yes ___ No ___

If yes, how? _____

_____

_____

If no, is there someone on my Recovery Team who might be able to help me address this resentment?

      Yes ___ No ___

If yes, who? _____

If no, whom could I talk to who might be willing to help me work on this resentment?

      Person:_____

6. Did I try to make someone else responsible for my Serenity this day?

      Yes ___ No ___

If yes, who? _____

      How did I try to make them responsible for my Serenity?

_____

_____

7. Did I do anything today which was harmful or hurtful?

      Yes ___ No ___ Uncertain ___

      If yes, was this towards a person or thing?

A. The person I hurt today was _____

_____

and how I harmed or hurt him/her was _____

_____._____

This happened because I _____

_____

B. The thing I harmed today was _____

and how I harmed or hurt this thing was _____

_____

This happened because I _____

_____

8. Can I think of a way to make amends for this error?

        Yes ___ No ___

If yes, how? _____

_____

_____

If no, is there someone on my Recovery Team who might be able to help me learn how to make amends for this error?

        Yes ___ No ___

If yes, who? _____

If no, whom could I talk to who might be willing to help me work on making amends for this error?

        Person: _____

9. What were my Affirmation and my Goal for today?

        (for suggestions see Step 6 on Healing)

My Affirmation for today was

_____

_____

My Goal for today was

_____

_____

What were the positive things I did today that helped me realize my Goal for today?

        A. _____
        B. _____

10. What will be my Affirmation and my Goal for tomorrow?

My Affirmation for tomorrow is

_____

_____

My Goal for tomorrow is

_____

_____

Step 11

◆

Seeking Serenity, Courage and Wisdom

We seek through prayer and meditation to improve conscious contact with our Higher Power, asking only for knowledge of His will for us in our adult lives.

If all humanity came from one place and we were all headed in exactly the same direction, then we would need only one spiritual path to follow. This, obviously, is not the case since we come from different lands and times with entirely unique life histories.

The 11th Step contains the challenging task of carving out the empty space necessary to experience serenity. This may be difficult as we are not sure how to develop this inner quiet. We cannot go from running full speed to sitting perfectly still, but there are ways for us to slow down. By becoming aware of serenity for a few moments in the morning or the evening, we will eventually carry this same sense of inner stillness with us into the rest of our day. This is an erratic process. At times our development is rapid, while at other times nothing seems to be happening at all.

Please do not feel that any one of the techniques offered in this chapter is greater or lesser than the others; they are simply different. I have organized them in the same manner they flowed during my working and reworking the 11th Step. Regardless of our spiritual origins, there are at least three common barriers to cultivating a relationship with our Higher Power: **chaos, attachment**, and **withdrawal**.

The Barrier of Chaos

True serenity may sound, at first, like a fantasy conjured up by a mystic group of glassy-eyed fanatics. The noise levels in our lives have been so loud for so long we may have adapted to living in chronic uproar. Our adaptation to continual chaos may be so accomplished that silence or stillness is threatening and uncomfortable.

While on retreat at the Abbey of Gethsemani, one man caught my eye. Throughout the entire time, he was on the move, either jogging along the road or riding the bicycle he brought with him. He made little noise to disturb the other guests, but always wore his headphones and portable tape player, even during meals. He was always the first to finish eating, since he ate with ferocity, and always the first to leave the chapel when services ended.

I checked with the guest master and he grinned when I asked about this fellow, since he, too, had noticed this behavior. He then told me how this particular individual had made a great effort, at no small expense, to come a far distance just to spend a few days at the Abbey. The guest master gently shook his head as he commented sadly, "I guess a lot of people don't know how to slow down. Maybe the inner silence, which is there for all of us, frightens them." I suspect he is right. I have often thought about that anonymous pilgrim, and how I am just like him sometimes.

The Barrier of Attachment

By remaining firmly attached to beliefs out of fear, rather than through conscious choice, we may fail to do the work required to develop an adult spirituality.[1] Attachment to religious stereotypes is another means of creating a barrier. Once we have been able to move beyond such stereotypes into a truly open dialogue, we may be pleasantly surprised by how much our spiritual experiences have in common.[2]

Carl Jung notes the critical differences between an external religious system which one joins much like a country club or political party, and a deep spiritual faith.[3] A country-club type of religious faith defines the things one must do and must not do, whereas the internal spiritual path is noted for the freedom it gives to love, grow, and change. In prayerfully considering our spirituality, we may find ourselves returning to the religious traditions we knew as children, or we may change religious traditions altogether.

The Barrier Of Withdrawal

Even after we have been able to push back the chaos and challenge our spiritual attachments, there still remains a formidable barrier to daily serenity: withdrawal.

Within several months after I started using the 12 Steps, I slowly began to experiment with a variety of meditation techniques under the guidance of several Recovery Team members. In doing so, however, some very strange things began to happen. I experienced heightened levels of irritability, increased episodes of free-floating anxiety and erratic mood fluctuations. There was also chronic restlessness plus such physical symptoms as heart palpitations, constipation, goose-bumps, chills, muscle twitches and even cramps. More disturbing were the ever worsening panic attacks and increased episodes of checking out.

During this time I was given a copy of Dr. Gerald May's landmark work, *Addiction and Grace*.[4] Within this text he weaves together neurology, addiction theory and spiritual teachings. In examining his book, many of the symptoms present in drug withdrawal seemed to fit my current situation, although I knew I was drug free. Still, there was this very strong intuition that the problem of chemical withdrawal applied to me: but how?

One day while looking through my 4th Step photo album, I glanced at a picture of myself taken about age 11 in which I appeared to be under the influence of some pretty heavy drugs: the vacant stare along with an "off in the ozone" grin. The abuse I was suffering at the time was horrific, so what could possibly explain this strange and incongruent image? Suddenly the connection between the child I was and my current symptoms became clear. When I was first sexually abused, a part of my brain automatically began to produce neurochemicals necessary to guard my immature mind from trauma. By age 30 I had survived on, and become addicted to, a complex host of self-produced pain killers, memory blockers, and emotional anesthetics. The techniques I had been employing to increase awareness were now directly challenging these neurological blocks. No wonder I was having withdrawal symptoms!

We know that individuals who have been dependent on drugs produced outside the body (alcohol, barbiturates, amphetamines, etc.) need to be closely monitored as they are detoxified from these drugs, especially if they have been chemically dependent for an extended period of time. If adult survivors are actually addicted to their own neurochemistry, it is imperative they be followed closely by Recovery Team members when working with any of the techniques presented here in the 11th Step. You can get into some very deep trouble quite rapidly if you go too far, too fast.

Quieting The Breath

There are several advantages to beginning a spiritual practice by working with breath. First, it is something we do naturally and the techniques can be employed anywhere at any time without complex training. Additionally, almost all religious traditions include at least a few breathing exercises as part of their teachings. Rather than attempt to describe all the techniques available for working with breath, I will offer a basic outline. One strategy is to put the word "Breathe" on a piece of paper where you will see it frequently as a reminder. Such places might include the bathroom mirror, the refrigerator door, a bulletin board, or on the dashboard of your car. You might also consider putting this reminder card in your briefcase or wallet.

170

While breathing is natural, we are rarely conscious of this fundamental physical process or the effects chronic hypervigilance has upon the muscles of the diaphragm. In working with my massage therapist, one of the first things which struck me was how rigid and inflexible my breathing muscles had become over the years. By becoming conscious of breath one learns to not only soften the muscles used in breathing, but eventually many other muscle groups throughout the entire body.

Once aware of our breathing patterns, we can continue to increase our mindfulness by counting the breaths we take (counting up to three, five, or ten for example). Once this number is reached we can then repeat the cycle until we have reached our allotted time limit. Some individuals find it helpful to use a string of rosary or prayer beads to keep track of their counting. Also, the tactile sensation of holding something in our hands may aid us in keeping our concentration focused.

Others may find the use of a repetitious prayer, or mantra, helpful. While there are many various prayers and mantras available, you might experiment with several (under the guidance of a Recovery Team Member) until you find those which most comfortably fit your individual style and spiritual path. While some prefer to practice with their eyes closed, others feel more comfortable with their eyes open. If you choose to work with this technique while your eyes are open, try to allow your vision to become gently unfocused. Generally, a person's attention tends to drift and wander more when their eyes are closed than when open; it is also easier to fall asleep with your eyes shut.

If you use any of these breathing techniques while sitting down, I suggest doing so no more than once in the morning and/or once in the evening for no more than five to ten minutes at a time. You might consider using a timer to help you keep track of your time limits. As simple as these techniques sound, they can be extremely difficult to master in the beginning. There are times when we need to gently nudge ourselves, but there are other times when pushing too hard is both unhelpful and unwise. A greater intensity of withdrawal symptoms may indicate a need to slow down and to give your nervous system time to adapt to this new level before continuing.

Walking With Mindfulness

I would highly recommend *A Guide to Walking Meditation* as a unique approach to spiritual growth for those of us who have difficulties with coordination and body awareness.[5] Walking is done for its own sake without specific geographical goal, in a place where we feel safe. If you choose walking meditation, practice without distraction in a quiet park, solitary lane or empty woods. Others may use an enclosed walking track or gymnasium, but regardless of location make sure it is a place where you feel secure. It is important to set limits either upon distance or time during these first sessions. Think in terms of a mile and/or 15 to 20 minutes. Frequency and time of day should fit individual needs and circumstances.

Practice walking with mindfulness. When you begin, gently focus upon each step, noticing how the sole of your foot feels as it touches the ground. As you continue, think about the negative emotions you may be carrying, such as anxiety or worry. Give yourself permission to let them go like rocks which drop from your hands, or cold rain drops falling from your clothes.

It may take many sessions before you can begin to walk with comfort and ease, but with experience you begin to notice a more harmonic rhythm of breath and step. As you develop mindfulness when walking, expand this awareness to the environment around you. Rather than stopping abruptly to stare at some tree or flower, slow your pace to take in the beauty while maintaining your rhythmic breathing pattern. Then, in a fluid and uninterrupted manner, resume your walk.

Sitting in Silence

Sitting meditation techniques are a powerful means for developing a sense of inner stillness and calm. However, it is very easy to overdo such work in the beginning unless we closely monitor ourselves and are under the supervision of a Recovery Team member trained in these techniques. If you have been in Recovery for only a short while, I would suggest you avoid a sitting practice at first and instead focus upon the breathing or walking.

For those who have been in Recovery for some time, and who feel attracted to this particular approach to working the 11th Step, I would like to make some cautionary remarks. The very act of practicing sitting meditation may increase the level of memory recall or flashbacks. Hence, this approach is probably not a good idea if you are already struggling with such problems. If you begin to have difficult memories when sitting in meditation, consider shifting your practice back to working with the breath or walking, and later return to sitting.

I was attempting to work with breath, walking and sitting techniques simultaneously before I realized how they can induce withdrawal symptoms. I thought I was making excellent progress until I noticed ever-worsening sensations of foreboding and agitation. However, I pressed on and continued to work with even more effort. The result of this ignorance was six to eight hours of continuous flashbacks and non-stop memory recall concerning dozens of abuse episodes. This horrific event put my Recovery back many months. If I had known then what I know now, I would have backed off immediately from working with all of these techniques at once. The overwhelming recall of that night was probably avoidable if I had listened to the signals indicative of neurochemical withdrawal that my body had been sending me during the previous weeks.

I found the following advice very helpful as I slowly returned to my daily meditations: Try to find a friendly and supportive group when you begin to practice any type of meditation. Avoid meditating when it is dark or gloomy. Be sure you do not attempt to sit for long periods of time, and keep in mind that any difficulty you have with recall or intense emotion is not your fault.[6] Both for my own sake, and the sake of those around me, I now tread much more cautiously, and gently, when practicing all of the 11th Step techniques.

Entering into Solitude

Of the many dangers deep sea divers face, the most serious is decompressing from great depths at too rapid a pace. This very serious problem, known as nitrogen narcosis or "the bends," causes great pain or even paralysis and can in some cases be life threatening. Those of us who have lived most of our lives under extraordinary emotional pressure, great physical stress, and chronic sensory overload can likewise develop serious decompression problems if we attempt to enter serenity and silence at too rapid a pace.

By realizing that we can decompress from noise and chaos too rapidly, we can make allowances for this when considering plans for a private retreat. Try to be realistic in considering how much time you wish to be alone. In the beginning you might try a one- or two-day retreat. One strategy is to allow yourself some time before the retreat to move gently into the quiet. When you return home, give yourself some additional space to allow the silence to remain with you just a little bit longer. This post-retreat time may be an excellent opportunity to reflect upon your time alone, or to review your retreat with a Recovery Team member while the experience is still fresh in your mind.

Another strategy to avoid decompression problems is to take with you a few things to occupy your mind when the silence and solitude become uncomfortable. If you feel you are getting into difficulties you can phone a Recovery Team member or talk with someone at the retreat facility. Always keep in mind that you have the absolute right to leave the retreat facility at any time for any reason.

Step 12

◆

New Life

Having had an adult spiritual awakening as a result of these Steps we try to carry to others our message of New Life through Healing. As a result of this awakening we try to practice the principals of strength, power, gentleness, and forgiveness with others in all our affairs.

As we consider the 12th Step, it would be easy to focus only upon words and social causes. However, when I think about the people who have had the greatest influence upon my Recovery, I remember most those individuals who embodied the spirit of the 12 Steps in their daily lives. It was not what they said which I remember, but who they were. Despite overwhelming pain and struggles, they courageously held on. I consider myself greatly blessed and deeply graced to have met those who had the great courage to transform their private Stumbling Blocks into Stepping Stones. In a similar manner, the strongest statement I can make is by practicing the principals of strength, power, gentleness, and forgiveness with others in all my affairs.

It would be an error to assume the presence of any Stumbling Block indicates we have failed in our previous Recovery efforts. This is simply not true. These Stumbling Blocks were, most likely, the very things which allowed us to survive. However, to transform them into Stepping Stones requires careful examination and patience. Stumbling Blocks can teach us many good lessons provided we are willing to work with them. If the following material applies to you, consider the resources of your Recovery Team. Rather than attempt to transform all of the Stumbling Blocks at once, pick the one you think will be easiest to change. This will help you gain the experience and wisdom necessary to successfully transform the next.

Transforming Self-Doubt into Self-Trust

We often express our fears by the questions we ask. For example, "If I was once in denial about my past, is it possible I might fall back into denial once again, and not know it?" It is healthy to ask such a question because it helps keep us honest with ourselves. We overcame our biggest denial when we took the First Step. As we completed each of the following Steps habitual patterns of denial were broken down even more. As long as we take time to listen to ourselves through our Daily Inventory, it is unlikely we will return to a permanent state of denial.

Another question we might ask is, "What if there are other memories of the abuse I have repressed and do not consciously recall? Will I be able to handle them in the future?" The answer to the first question is, yes. It is possible there are things you may not yet remember. If you doubt your being able to handle new memories of the past, remember you have already gained invaluable experience in handling this type of crisis.

Transforming Compulsions into Choices

As children, the coping skills we had available to us were extremely limited (such as denial, perfectionism, caretaking, acting-out, or over-eating). We learned how to be experts at using these few tools in order to survive. By the time we became adults our expertise in these matters was truly masterful. The problem is we no longer think about how we will act. Instead, when under stress, we fall back into old patterns which are safe and familiar.

We can use our old tools to help us build new tools. We take the time to think about what we are doing, and consider the resources available to us. When we are not sure if our familiar habits will work, we can explore alternative solutions and new strategies with our Recovery Team. Failure today is not always a life-and-death matter. Without panic or hysteria, we can begin to do things simply because we **want to** do them rather than because we **have to** do them. We are reclaiming our divine right to learn, think, and choose.

Transforming Hypervigilance into Awareness

Without realizing it, many of us developed an extraordinary ability to be aware of what was happening around us. Failure to maintain this almost telepathic state of hypervigilance was to be caught off guard by our abusers. We were never taught how to discern the differences between what we are really responsible for and what we are not. We continue to operate out of a position that we are responsible for everybody and everything all the time. Retraining ourselves to relax is not easy: just because we are aware of something does not automatically mean we are responsible. We learn the lesson of loving detachment.

Transforming Fragmentation into Critical Thinking

How many times have you been asked, "How do you feel about this-or-that?" or "What do you think about such-and-such?" only to go totally blank? Probably plenty of times. It is often frustrating to the people around us because they really do want to listen to us, and maddening to ourselves because we are not sure why we shut down. Rather than having no feelings or thoughts at all, my guess is we have too many reactions at once.

As children we had to develop an extraordinary ability to cope with a multitude of highly conflicting tasks. A part of us learned how to deny our feelings, and another part of us had to keep those same feelings under control at all times. One part of us had to be constantly on alert for what was happening around us. Another part had to keep up the façade that everything was fine. Some inner self had to think about what might happen next. At the same time another aspect of ourselves maintained our denial about what had happened in the past. Our psyches wanted to give up and die, even as we struggled against these same suicidal impulses.

By resolving our underlying conflicts the confusion levels will drop, and we gain a new level of clarity. This does not mean we will be able to discern "good" feelings from "bad," nor "right" thoughts from "wrong" ones. Thoughts are just thoughts, and feelings are just feelings. As children, we tend to view the world in simplistic, black and white terms. As adults, however, we know reality is often paradoxical and complex. We know what we see depends upon how we look at it.

When we decontaminate lives of confusion, we find we have the energy and the space to think clearly, maybe for the first time. We plan how to solve a particular problem, or how to avoid it. As we expand the number of options available, we look for the ones with the highest probability of success.

Transforming Asexuality/Hypersexuality into Intimacy

Because of childhood sexual abuse, many survivors experience a great deal of confusion concerning intimacy or sexuality— sometimes both. We hold the mistaken idea that all intimacy is bad, and or we may attempt to meet our emotional needs only in a sexual manner. Some of us try to disconnect ourselves from our sexuality because initial sexual experiences were so extremely traumatic, and we become non-sexual, or asexual. Others of us learned the only way to be close to someone was through the sexual act, knowing no other way to express care and love except by sharing our bodies. In this case we became hypersexual. At times we may swing from one extreme to the other, never finding a middle ground.

We can transform this Stumbling Block into a Stepping Stone when we begin to see relationships, not through the eyes of our wounded child, but rather with the eyes of our mature selves in Recovery. At first, in many ways we may be just as ignorant about sexuality or intimacy as any small child or young adolescent. We may still relate to ourselves, and others, on such a level. If the person who harmed us was male, then we will be afraid of our own masculine sexuality as we have only seen its dark side in others. If the one who abused us was female, we may be afraid of those aspects of ourselves which are feminine. In either case, we have become unbalanced in a multitude of ways. We may fear we will allow ourselves to be harmed as we once were in the past and never give ourselves permission to say "Yes." If we are afraid to be sexually assertive, we never have learned how to say "No!", even when it is in our best interest. Another imbalance is when we have had a number of sexual experiences, but never known gentleness and emotional intimacy.

Our greatest fear is that we will become like those who abused us. This fear prevents us from finding a healthy equilibrium; yet, if we work through our fears concerning sexuality and intimacy, we begin to find a more comfortable balance with ourselves and then with others. It is very important we remind ourselves again and again we have the right to choose how we will, and will not, address this Stumbling Block. We have the right to decide when and with whom we will discuss these matters.

Transforming Paranoia into Fellowship

Many times our fear assumes a distinctly paranoid quality, as there was a very real basis for this terrified stance in the past. We did not just think someone was out to get us; they were. We had concrete evidence to support our fears. Because of this, we had to find some way to feel safe, and in control. Those who were supposed to care for us failed. It was up to us to figure out how to survive as best we could, and we did. Our watchwords became: "Do not trust," "Do not move," "Do not let anyone get close," "Watch out for the warning signs that it might happen again," "Keep your guard up," "Do not let anyone touch you," "Do whatever you have to do to be safe!" Our childhood paranoia, once unquestionably necessary for physical survival, now imprisons us. The idea of letting someone close to us is terrifying. As adults in Recovery we can begin to think about moving beyond the walls of our defenses.

When we eventually do take our first tentative steps outside ourselves, we begin to discover something. We see others who were wounded, survived, and are healing. We might learn from them if we allow ourselves to get close enough to hear what they have to say. We may even be surprised to discover they are learning from us! When we can push ourselves through the anxiety of being touched, there is much healing in the simple act of letting someone hold our hand, maybe for the first time in years. In taking the immense risk of venturing beyond our walls, we discover we are not alone. We begin to find a true fellowship based on the common goals of Recovery.

Transforming Crisis Management into Creative Growth

For years our inner wounded child has demanded safety and security at any price. At the same time there were others who demanded we fulfill their expectations as well. We had to figure out some way of doing both things at once. Much of our turmoil, chaos and confusion arises from our success in doing just that. Everybody wanted something from us, and they wanted it "Now!" People yelled, "Jump!" and we asked, "How high?" We became extremely good at crisis management.

Feelings of hopelessness about the future kept us from believing we could live our lives in any other manner. Why should we plan for tomorrow's growth if we are afraid we cannot make it through the disasters of today? But, as we continue to follow our Recovery, the fears of our wounded child will slowly subside as he becomes stronger and learns how to say "No!" to the demands of others. We begin to move past the driven need to find a one-time-cure-all-miracle to our problems. We let go of the false belief we have to find "The Solution," "The Truth," "The Teacher," or "The Path" in order to survive.

We can move beyond our daily, hand-to-hand combat with the past through evolving discipline, patience, and determination. Somewhere in the fight we realize that our own private war is over. There are still battles to wage, but we are finally winning!

Transforming Mourning into Thankfulness

We naturally go through a type of "What if . . ." or "If only . . ." thinking as we grieve the many losses caused by childhood abuse. We may find ourselves wondering, "What if I had not been in denial all those years . . .", or, "If only I knew then what I know now . . ." Such thoughts are necessary for they help us to grieve the past, and to move toward the future.

It would be very easy to allow our much-needed mourning to become a bottomless black hole of grief simply because we are afraid we will never be able to move past the losses. If we focus **only** upon those things which should have been, or never were, we are in danger of becoming stuck. If we allow feelings of despair or self-blame to fill our minds completely, we run the risk of becoming ensnared by our resentments and anger.

Thinking honestly, we need to ask a second set of "What if . . ." and "If only . . ." questions. "What if I had never begun my Recovery at all?" "What if I had acted differently?" "How could things have gone worse than they did?" "If I had not made any changes in my life at all, where would I be now?"

Sometimes it takes a great deal of energy to keep a focus on the good in life. The "maybes" and "could have beens" are extremely painful sometimes. I often have to deliberately remind myself that now is now, and yesterday was yesterday.

The Serenity Prayer

God grant me the Serenity
to accept the things I cannot change,
the Courage to change the things I can,
and the Wisdom to know the difference.
      — *Reinhold Niebuhr*

To allow oneself to be carried away by a
multitude of conflicting concerns, to
surrender to too many demands, to commit
oneself to too many projects, to
want to help everyone in everything,
is to succumb to violence.
      — *Thomas Merton*

Epilogue

◆

Life After The 12 Steps

In the beginning as I struggled with my own Recovery, I would from time to time catch only the rarest glimpses of the land just beyond the 12 Steps. Gradually over the past few years, I have found myself living more fully in that realm. As I continue to enter into this new domain, I have discovered that I am letting go not only the pains of the past, but also, strangely enough, even the 12 Steps themselves. At first, this destination may appear a bit boring from the outside, especially after the battles we have had to fight in order to find our wounded inner child, to heal him, and then to be at one with him within ourselves. Sometimes, it is even a little scary coming to this place since at first it seems so utterly foreign and unfamiliar. Yet, there is an unmistakable knowing deep down in the bones this reclaimed soil is home.

In this new country our friends and music are celebrated as equally, and as thankfully, as is our solitude and silence. Here is the safe sanctuary where our wives or partners are watched with gentle eyes, touched with strong hands, and whispered to quietly. The bills are paid, the car is washed, and meals are cooked. It is a place where there are just things to do. Yet, in the doing it is also a realm of infinite wonder, endless newness, delightful surprises and the most subtle of joys. In this valley the once separate streams of Work and Grace, Faith and Action converge, and begin to flow as one continuous river. It is a place of restful sleep, and in the end, which is only another beginning, a peaceful death. This landscape has been described by any number of names. Some know it as Serenity. Others experience it as Enlightenment. Still others describe it as The Here And Now. By whatever name you choose to know it, may it be yours.

**When the house is finished, it is time
to put down the tools.**
— TLS

Notes

Introduction. THE NEED FOR THE 12 STEPS OF RECOVERY

    1. Charles L. Whitfield, *Healing the Child Within* (Gig Harbor, Washington: HealthComm, Inc., 1987).
    2. Mike Lew, *Victims No Longer: Men Recovering from Incest and Other Sexual Child Abuse* (New York: Harper & Row, 1990), pages 152-153.
    3. Sandra Butler, *Conspiracy of Silence:The Trauma of Incest* (Volcano, California: Volcano Pr., Inc., 1985), pages 3-17.
    4. John Bradshaw, *Healing the Shame That Binds You* (Gig Harbor, Washington: HealthComm, Inc., 1988), pages 48-50.
    5. Ellen Bass & Laura Davis, *Courage to Heal: A Guide for Women Survivors of Child Sexual Abuse* (New York: Harper & Row, 1988), pages 13-18.

Chapter 3. THE RECOVERY JOURNAL
    1. Ira Progoff, *At a Journal Workshop:The Basic Text & Guide for Using the Intensive Journal Process* (New York: Dialogue House, 1975), pages 9-15.
    2. Stephen LeBerge, *Lucid Dreaming* (New York: Ballentine Books, Inc., 1986).

Chapter 4. STEP 1 — ACKNOWLEDGMENT
    1. American Psychiatric Association: *Diagnostic and Statistical Manual of Mental Disorders, Third Addition, Rev.* (Washington, D.C.: American Psychiatric Association, 1987), pages 247-251.
    2. Elizabeth Kubler-Ross, *On Death & Dying* (New York: Macmillan, 1970).
    3. David Grove Seminars: *Healing the Wounded Child Within* (Edwardsville, Illinois: 1989).

Chapter 4. STEP 2 — BELIEF
    1. Father Leonard Loegering, Unpublished Works, (Pisek, North Dakota:St. John's Nepomucene Church).
    2. Loegering, Ibid.
    3. Loegering, Ibid.
    4. Loegering, Ibid.
    5. Loegering, Ibid.
    6. Eugene Monick, *Phallos: sacred image of the masculine* (Toronto: Inner City Books, 1987), pages 39-42.

7. Loegering, Ibid.

8. Joseph Campbell, *Hero with a Thousand Faces* (Princeton: Princeton University Press, 1990).

9. Kahlil Gibran, *The Prophet* (New York: Knopf, 1966), pages 39-43.

STEP 3 — AWARENESS

1. DSM-III-R, Ibid.

2. Norman Cousins, *Anatomy of an Illness As Perceived by the Patient: Reflections on Healing & Regeneration* (New York: Norton, 1979), pages 27-48.

3. Erik H. Erikson, *Childhood & Society* (New York: Norton, 1986).

STEP 5 — ADMISSION

1. Bill Moyers & Robert Bly, *A Gathering of Men* (Public Affairs Television, 356 W 58th St., New York, 1990).

STEP 7 — FORGIVENESS

1. Stephen Levine, *A Gradual Awakening* (New York: Anchor Press, 1979), pages 53-56, 85-90.

2. Stephen Levine, *Meetings At The Edge* (Garden City: Anchor Press, 1984), page ix (Introduction).

3. Rabbi Harold S. Kushner, *When Bad Things Happen To Good People* (New York: Avon, 1981), page 139.

STEP 8 — SPECIFYING AMENDS

1. Melody Beattie, *Codependent No More: How to Stop Controlling Others & Start Caring for Yourself* (New York: Harper Row, 1988).

2. Robin Norwood, *Women Who Love Too Much:When You Keep Wishing and Hoping He'll Change* (Los Angeles: J.P. Tarcher, 1985).

STEP 11 — SEEKING SERENITY, COURAGE AND WISDOM

1. M. Scott Peck, *Road Less Traveled* (New York: Simon & Schuster, 1988).

2. Susan Walker, editor, *Speaking of Silence: Christians and Buddhists on the Contemplative Way* (Mahwah: Paulist Press, 1987).

3. Carl G. Jung, *Undiscovered Self* (New York: New American Library, 1974).

4. Gerald C. May, *Addiction & Grace* (New York: Harper Row, 1990), pages 1-20.

5. Nhat Hanh Thich, *Guide to Walking Meditation* (Nyack: Fellowship of Reconciliation, 1985).

6. Reverend Donald Gilbert, private correspondence, used with permission.

Support Groups

There are any number of support groups available to survivors which specifically address the issue of childhood sexual abuse. Some survivors may find working with such support groups to be a very powerful tool for healing. For others, however, such support groups are not a viable option for any number of reasons (i.e., distance to travel, time limitations, stage of Recovery, etc.). My own personal feelings about all support groups goes back to the old adage of going with what works best for you, and doing those things which are comfortable for you. The list given here for abuse survivors support groups is by no means intended to be comprehensive. For additional information about such groups, I would refer the reader to both *Victims No Longer* as well as *The Courage to Heal*.

Incest Survivors Anonymous
> I.S.A. World Service Office
> Post Office Box 5613
> Long Beach, CA 90805
> A 12-Step fellowship for both male and female survivors of sexual abuse. Literature available.

Survivors of Incest Anonymous
> S.I.A. World Service Office
> Post Office Box 21817
> Baltimore, MA 21222
> A 12-Step fellowship for both male and female survivors of sexual abuse. Literature available.

P.L.E.A. (Prevention, Leadership, Education, Assistance)
> P.L.E.A.
> Post Office Box 6545
> Santa Fe, NM 87502
> (505) 982-9184
> Founded by Hank Estrada, this organization is dedicated to offering information and support for non-offending male survivors. Literature available.

Safer Society Program and Press
   The Safer Society Program
   Rural Route 1, Box 24-B
   Orwell, VT 05760
   (802) 897-7541
   Directed by Fay Honey Knopp, this organization focuses upon providing publications and referrals for both male and female survivors and offenders.

Suggested Readings

The following group of suggested Readings is highly subjective and personal. The titles listed here are those which I have found most helpful over the course of my Recovery. If there is a particular Life Area you find especially difficult, consider starting with some of those works listed in that area. Also, I have attempted to offer alternative support groups for the various Life Areas when possible.

Suggested Readings — The Psychologial Life Area

Franklin Abbott, Editor, *Men And Intimacy: Personal Accounts Exploring the Dilemmas of Modern Male Sexuality*. Freedom, California: The Crossing Press, 1990. A provocative collection of articles, poetry, essays and biography which address a wide range of men's issues. The topics range from male rape to homophobia, sexual abuse to patriarchy.

John Bradshaw, *Bradshaw On: Healing The Shame That Bind You*. Deerfield Beach, Florida: Health Communications, 1988. Based upon the work of Gershan Kaufman, Bradshaw explores the insidious and toxic influences of childhood shame upon adult living. Not only does he detail the means of recognizing such shame, he goes the next step and offers ways of healing from it.

Viktor E. Frankl, *Man's Search for Meaning*. New York: Simon and Schuster, 1963. First published in 1939. This is a moving account of one Nazi death camp survivor's struggles to again find personal meaning when all he has ever loved has been destroyed.

Stephen LeBerge, *Lucid Dreaming*. New York: Ballentine Books, 1986. Written by a leading expert in the area of sleep disorders and sleep research. The research offered is compelling in addition to many practical suggestions on how to learn lucid dreaming.

Alice Miller, *The Drama of the Gifted Child.* New York: Basic Books, 1981. Miller reveals in this text (originally published in German in 1979) how narcissistic parents both form and deform the emotional, psychological and spiritual lives of their gifted children.

Eugene Monick, *Phallos: sacred image of the masculine.* Toronto: Inner City Books, 1987. Written within the context of Jungian psychology, this text openly explores the depth dynamics of masculinity. Due to the subject matter and the graphic nature of the text, this book could be disturbing to some survivors.

Ira Progoff, *At A Journal Workshop: The basic text and guide for using the Intensive Journal process.* New York: Dialogue House Library, 1975. This is most likely the book which sparked my Recovery.

Mike Samuels and Nancy Samuels, *Seeing With The Mind's Eye: The History, Techniques and Uses of Visualization.* Berkeley: The Bookworks, 1975. A comprehensive and beautifully illustrated text addressing visualization as both a healing and problem solving technique.

Other Support Groups to Consider:
Emotions Anonymous
National Alliance for the Mentally Ill (NAMI)
2101 Wilson Boulevard, Suite 302
Arlington, Virginia   22201

Suggested Readings — The Spiritual Life Area

Patricia Christian-Meyer, *Catholic America.* Sante Fe, New Mexico: John Muir Publications, 1989. A comprehensive directory of over 600 self-renewal centers and retreat facilities in the United States and Canada.

Harold S. Kushner *When Bad Things Happen To Good People.* New York: Avon Books, 1981. Written from the heart after his only son died at age 14 of progeria, "rapid aging." Out of great pain comes a clear vision of continued life and love.

Stephen Levine, *A Gradual Awakening.* New York: Anchor Press, 1979. Over the past years this book has shown me that there really is such a thing as Serenity. Regardless of your spritual orientation, I suspect Levine may have something to say to you.

Don Morreale, editor, *Buddhist America Centers, Retreats, Practices.* Santa Fe, New Mexico: John Muir Publications, 1988. Describes over 500 Theravada, Mahayana, Vajrayana, and nonsectarian facilities, their practices and styles of retreat.

Nhat Hanh Thich, *Guide to Walking Meditation*. Nyack, New York: Fellowship of Reconciliation, 1985. Written by a Vietnamese monk who has seen more death than one could ever imagine. Yet, despite all the many losses this man has experienced, his words still are filled with deep laughter and honest joy.

M. Basil Pennington, O.C.S.O. *A Place Apart: Monastic Prayer for Everyone*. Garden City, New York: Doubleday & Company, 1983. A good place to begin if you are learning how to carve out some silence and solitude on a daily basis.

Ira Progoff, *The Practice of Process Meditation: The Intensive Journal Way to Spiritual Experience*. New York: Dialogue House Library, 1980. Time and time again, there are new things to learn every time I open this book. A nondenominational approach to spiritual growth.

Susan Walker, editor, *Speaking of Silence: Christians & Buddhists on the Comtemplative Way*. Mahwah, New Jersey: Paulist Press, 1987. It is amazing how much those of a contemplative spiritual experience have in common. This book contains any number of perspectives, ideas, and opinions which are rarely heard within many mainstream denominations. Recommended highly.

Suggested Readings — The Sexual Life Area

Ellen Bass and Laura Davis, *The Courage to Heal: A Guide for Women Survivors of Child Sexual Abuse*. New York: Harper & Row, 1988. While written specifically for female survivors, many of the exercises are equally practical for men. Excellent resource listing at back of book.

Sandra Butler, *Conspiracy of Silence: The Trauma of Incest*. Volcano, California: Volcano Press, 1978, 1985. Considered by many to be the book which forever broke the taboo of discussing something no one previously had wanted to discuss.

Laura Davis, *The Courage to Heal Workbook: For Women and Men Survivors of Child Sexual Abuse*. New York: Harper & Row, 1990. What I like about this workbook is how easily the author allows the reader to set their own time limits.

Eliana Gil, Ph.D. *Outgrowing the Pain: A Book For And About Adults Abused As Children*. Walnut Creek, California: Launch Press, 1983. Clear, simple, practical and, most of all, short. The subjects are broken down into small sections. This is especially helpful for those survivors who have difficulty with dissociation.

Mic Hunter, *Abused Boys: The Neglected Victims of Sexual Abuse*. Lexington, Massachusetts: Lexington Books, 1990. A very well researched text with an extensive and impressive bibliography.

Mike Lew, *Victims No Longer: Men Recovering from Incest and Other Sexual Child Abuse.* New York: Harper & Row, 1990. When I first saw this book I got goosebumps. When I first read this book I cried. Now when I read this book I see how far I've come. Excellent resource listing at back of book.

T. Thomas, *Men Surviving Incest: A Male Survivor Shares the Process of Recovery.* Walnut Creek, California: Launch Press, 1989. Powerful and compelling reading. An honest and intimate sharing of one man's struggles to heal through and beyond the past.

Other Support Groups To Consider:
Sex Addicts Anonymous

Suggested Readings — The Physical Life Area

Alcoholics Anonymous, *Alcoholics Anonymous* (a.k.a. "The Big Blue Book"). New York, New York: Alcoholics Anonymous World Services, Inc., 1976. The history of the grandparent of all 12-Step Recovery Programs. Includes personal accounts of alcohol Recovery.

Bob Anderson, *Stretching.* Boninas, California: Shelter Publications, 1980. I especially like his approach to physical health: go slow, go easy, don't hurt yourself, and have some fun! A useful book to help survivors reconnect with their bodies in a nonthreatening and safe manner.

Norman Cousins, *Anatomy of an Illness As Perceived by the Patient: Reflections on Healing and Regeneration.* New York, New York: Norton, 1986. What you think can make you sick. What you think can make you well. An extraordinary personal testimony to the power of healing.

Elisabeth Kübler-Ross, *On Death and Dying.* New York, New York: MacMillan, 1970. Ever since it was first published, this text has touched millions of lives. Death does not end a relationship, it simply changes it.

Stephen Levine, *Meetings At The Edge.* Garden City, New York: Anchor Press, 1984. Healing does not always mean that your disease will be cured. This text has as much to say to those who do not know they are dying as it does to those who do.

Gerald C. May, *Addiction and Grace.* New York, New York: Harper and Row, 1990. May does a most impressive job of weaving together in a readable work neurological research, psychology and spirituality. What is especially refreshing is his honesty concerning his own struggles in the search for grace.

Sondra Ray, *The Only Diet There Is.* Berkeley, California: Celestial Arts, 1981. A loving and compassionate exploration of eating disorders. Simple, yet clear. The affirmation exercises are especially good.

Hans Selye, *The Stress Of Life*. New York, New York: McGraw-Hill Book Company, 1978. First released in 1956 and revised since then, it is considered by many to be the first text to scientifically explore the connection between illness and stress. Certain passages of this book do tend to become a bit technical.

Other Support Groups to Consider:
Alcoholics Anonymous (A.A.)
Narcotics Anonymous (N.A.)
National Hospice Organization
1901 North Moore Street, Suite 901
Arlington, Virginia 22209
Overeaters Anonymous (O.A.)

Suggested Readings — The Social Life Area

Alan Arkin, *The Lemming Condition*. New York, New York: Harper and Row, 1976. While written as a children's book, it still has something to say to anyone who realizes that they live in a world which is out of control.

James P. Carse, *Finite and Infinite Games: A Vision of Life as Play and Possibility*. New York, New York: The Free Press, 1986. The goal of a finite game is to determine a winner and a loser at the end of the game. The goal of an infinite game, on the other hand, it to continue the game. A thought-provoking work.

Erik H. Erickson, *Childhood and Society*. New York, New York: Norton, 1986. A truly landmark text on the social development of childhood. Definitely recommended reading for anyone interested in knowing more about the struggles and tasks of becoming fully human and humane.

Daniel J. Levinson, et. al., *The Seasons of a Man's Life*. New York, New York: Knopf, 1978. An indepth exploration of those tasks and conflicts with which men struggle. A helpful text to anyone who wants to know more about adult male stages of development.

Judith Viorst, *Necessary Losses: The Loves, Illusions, Dependencies and Impossible Expectations That All of Us Have to Give Up in Order to Grow*. New York, New York: Ballantine Books, 1986. To grow is to gain, but in gaining there is also loss. A thorough examination of those things of which we must let go in order to become ourselves.

Robert Jay Lifton, *Death In Life: Survivors of Hiroshima*. New York, New York: Simon and Schuster, 1967. As the bumper-sticker says, "Nuclear War Is The Ultimate Form Of Child Abuse!" This book proves it. I dare anyone to tell me that they are the same after having read this work.

190

Other Support Groups to Consider:
   Adult Children Anonymous (support for those from any dysfunctional family of origin)
   Al-Anon (for friends and family of an alcoholic)

Suggested Readings — The Economic Life Area

Richard Nelson Bolles, *What Color Is Your Parachute?: A Practical Manual for Job Hunters and Career Changers.* Berkley: Ten-Speed Press, 1983. If you want to find a job, change jobs, switch careers, or just get a better handle on what makes you special, take a look at this landmark text. Consistently gets great reviews every time it is reissued and updated.

Consumer Reports Magazine. Do you know what used automobile to buy (or not buy)? What refrigerator is the least expensive to both purchase and operate? How do you choose one product over another? This magazine can easily pay for the subscription price in one year. Spend smart - you could use the money you save elsewhere!

Sylvia Porter, *Sylvia Porter's Your Financial Security: Making Your Money Work at Every Stage of Your Life.* New York: Avon Books, 1990. This author has the extraordinary ability to make the complicated uncomplicated. Practical, realistic financial advice. Has been around for years, and with good reason.

Marsha Sinetar, *Do What You Love, The Money Will Follow: Discovering Your Right Livelihood.* New York: Dell Publishing, 1989. An interesting integration of spirituality and economics. Practical advice with a soul.

Other Support Groups to Consider:
   Debtors Anonymous
   Gamblers Anonymous